FROM THE LIBRARY OF
BERKELEY COLLEGE

New York:
NYC Midtown
Brooklyn • White Plains

New Jersey:
Clifton • Dover • Newark • Paramus
Woodbridge • Woodland Park

Berkeley College Online:
BerkeleyCollege.edu/Online

The Rise of the Curator Class

The Rise of the Curator Class

Changing the Way We Buy, Sell, and Make Everything

Steffon Davis

 PRAEGER™

An Imprint of ABC-CLIO, LLC
Santa Barbara, California • Denver, Colorado

Library of Congress Cataloging-in-Publication Data

Names: Davis, Steffon, author.
Title: The rise of the curator class : changing the way we buy, sell, and make everything/Steffon Davis.
Description: Santa Barbara, CA : Praeger, [2019] | Includes bibliographical references and index.
Identifiers: LCCN 2018053020 (print) | LCCN 2018055740 (ebook) | ISBN 9781440860508 (ebook) | ISBN 9781440860492 (cloth : alk. paper)
Subjects: LCSH: Technological innovations—Economic aspects. | Information technology—Economic aspects.
Classification: LCC HC79.T4 (ebook) | LCC HC79.T4 .D386 2019 (print) | DDC 338—dc23
LC record available at https://lccn.loc.gov/2018053020

ISBN: 978-1-4408-6049-2 (print)
     978-1-4408-6050-8 (ebook)

23 22 21 20 19   1 2 3 4 5

This book is also available as an eBook.

Praeger
An Imprint of ABC-CLIO, LLC

ABC-CLIO, LLC
147 Castilian Drive
Santa Barbara, California 93117
www.abc-clio.com

This book is printed on acid-free paper ∞

Manufactured in the United States of America

Contents

Preface

Think of the stuff you love most: clothes, games, cars, or artwork. One night a genie grants you unlimited ownership to as much of it as you can imagine. How incredible would that be? A feast of everything you love.

That's what it felt like in 1999 as a music-loving teenager using the music file-sharing service Napster. That Christmas, I had just asked for two music albums. Then one piece of software later, I was downloading every album I could think of from the Internet. It was sheer bliss, an endless Christmas morning whereby the number of presents was limited only by the length of my wish list.

But as with all genies, this one had a catch (besides Napster's illegality and eventual shutdown). After gorging euphorically on the music I already knew, I didn't know what to download next. It's as if Napster said "the musical universe is yours!" but only provided a map to places I'd already been. It didn't make sense; how could "everything" be available—with the implication that there would always be something new and amazing to listen to—yet I remained stuck in the same musical corner? The search bar, the heretofore king of retrieving what I wanted online, now mocked me. The problem was that I didn't know what I wanted; I'd need to hear it first.

There was one work-around, however; it was possible to search for music I already liked and then browse the entire music collection of the person sharing it. Sometimes this led to great new discoveries (most of the time it didn't). But when it worked, it really worked and provided a fresh injection of musical bliss. It also taught me that while the Napster software itself didn't have the right features to help me discover something new, other people using it could.

As the Internet continued to rocket the world and global economy into the future, more and more content came online, and the problem of discovery that affected music sharing started to overwhelm other categories as well—everything from e-commerce to video to the news. Today the crisis of discovery is at a fever pitch, as people who want to find content they like can't.

Makers struggle to be discovered at all. And the tools that are supposed to help us instead fail, some with serious, unintended global consequences—#FakeNews—that we'll get into later. At the same time, information technology continues to advance, and when its creators are faced with the problems it creates, they often respond that the solution is in fact more technology.

For the past 10 years, I've worked with cutting-edge technologies as both an entrepreneur and a product manager in fields including self-driving cars, high-frequency trading, and recommendation engines. Across all of them, which involve big data and algorithm development, I've noticed that these seemingly "objective" disciplines are bathed in human subjectivity. For example, with self-driving vehicles, it's not enough to design a car that drives in isolation (or even among other robot cars); rather, it must accommodate the subjectivity of all the drivers, pedestrians, bicyclists, and motorcyclists encountered (e.g., how fast is a comfortable lane change for the passenger as well as for the pedestrians?). With high-frequency stock trading, it may seem like an entirely rational activity. After all, it's computers trading stocks, and all they have to do is buy low and sell high. In reality, however, the algorithms always buy and sell from either human traders or from other algorithms designed by humans, each of whom have their own point of view of what is considered high or low (and they get it wrong a lot). In the world of technology, it's not turtles all the way down; it's actually humans all the way down.

While working in these fields (especially recommendation engines), I studied human subjectivity from both a social science and a computer science point of view to better develop an edge in my work, translating and evolving preexisting theory and research into something pragmatic that could be programmed. Simultaneously, in the broader industry and media environment, the topic of curation rose in prominence with seemingly everything becoming curated, from the ingredients in your salad to the iPhone App Store. And while the word "curation" can be overused to the point of losing all meaning (we will lock down a useful definition shortly), at a broad level it's most often used to describe the taste-based point of view that people bring to buying, selling, and making everything in a hyperefficient economy currently designed more for efficiency than delight. In many ways, curation has taken the shape of a countermovement against technorational digitization, demanding that the emotional, human element return to our daily experience. Curation has also developed into a popular activity, as we've witnessed the rise of hundreds of millions of curators across the web transforming the Internet into more of a place they like to be. And with this new behavior, like new behaviors before it such as blogging and social networking, it has created a new class of actors with their own desires, logic, and business impact. With the curation genie out of the bottle, it's a question not of if the curator class will affect you and your business but rather how it already is. Welcome to the rise of the curator class.

Acknowledgments

This book was made possible with the support of my brother-in-law Daniel Nayeri, whose infectious, anything-is-possible attitude is only surpassed by his creativity and generosity. Thank you to my agent, Leah Spiro, and editor, Hilary Claggett, for believing in the vision and impact of curation. I'm especially grateful to my sister, mom, and dad, whose endless encouragement keep me afloat. And a debt of gratitude goes to my friend Dr. Isao Jonathan Sakata, whom I'm deeply fortunate to have had as a teacher and who taught me that questions are far more interesting than answers.

Introduction

Today's Internet is an "everything in the world" Internet. It's almost beyond our imagination. Anything that anyone in the world could ever hope to buy, listen to, read, or watch can be found, right at our fingertips.

The Internet is also an overwhelming fire hose of content responsible for the content overload epidemic.

Yet some people have learned to thrive in this climate of superabundance. Their secret? To tackle the overload and make sense of it for others. They're part of a new class of Internet citizen—the curator class—whose influence and power grow as more people look to them as guides. They're enabled by many of the world's largest tech companies, including Google, Apple, and Pinterest, that are learning to harness their passions. And the curator class is ushering in a new era whereby making new content is less essential than making sense of it.

This new curator class is also sweeping traditional curators into the dustbin of history. Curators have always done the heavy lifting of discovering and making sense of things. Whether it's a magazine editor selecting designs for an issue, a retailer choosing merchandise for a store, a radio DJ crafting a playlist, a TV producer programming a channel, a book editor acquiring manuscripts, or an art dealer creating a gallery, curators are on the front line of culture, discovering, contextualizing, and vetting content for the rest of us. This kind of curation used to be available to the elite few.

Now, Internet platforms such as Pinterest, Spotify, and Twitter empower hundreds of millions of people to curate their ideas for anyone who may be interested. This new curator class is producing tens of millions of organized, human-powered recommendations. Similar to a previous era when independent bookstore owners could provide personal, informed book recommendations and when record store employees could personally guide you to new music, curation reinvents discovery for the digital age—disrupting traditional gatekeepers and growing at a scale not seen since the invention of blogging.

Curation is set to overturn the $2.2 trillion global creative industry, revolutionizing how we create, market, and discover content. Whereas today's tools force consumers to either wade through endless oceans of unknown content or appeal to top 10 lists aimed at the lowest common denominator, a curated experience makes likable content find you. For creators, it allows for success outside the manic extremes of superstardom and obscurity, growing a healthy middle ground of niche markets. And it revolutionizes how content is sold as consumer trust moves further away from traditional brands and toward the curators who lead tastes.

But to understand the rise of the curator class, we have to understand the problems they're rising to solve: content overload.

PART 1

The Rise
of the Curator Class

Introduction to Part I
Content Overload

More content is produced every day than a person can consume in a lifetime. From snaps in Snapchat, pins in Pinterest, and instas from Instagram, the sheer number of options available to the average person is overwhelming. Unsurprisingly, feeling overloaded with content is the new normal. However, even with this proliferation, instead of distancing ourselves we have welcomed the content explosion with open arms. We expect there to be 100 different flavors of coffee at our local café, 1,000 types of baby strollers on Amazon, and 10,000 titles on Netflix, all with the option to browse and research for days on end to pick out our favorites. And as anyone who has put a video on YouTube, written a blog, or marketed an online business can attest to, content creators are in the same mess. With an endlessly growing sea of content, it's increasingly difficult to be discovered at all.

Clay Shirky (Internet smart guy) once said that content overload occurs when filters stop working.[1] And some of our most obvious filters—search engines, social networks, and recommendation algorithms—no longer work like we need them to. As a result, discovering content and products on our phones and laptops can feel overwhelming and downright frustrating.

Fundamentally, filters organize stuff in ways we could do ourselves. I could alphabetize a list of 1,000 strollers, but I'm glad I don't have to. I could sort them by lowest to highest price, but I've never had to do it manually. I could sort them by the ones I like most to the ones I like least, but, oh wait, there's no drop-down menu for that. I absolutely still do that by myself. It's as if the entire Internet zips around on a spaceship, but when it comes to finding what we like, we're still taking the stairs.

It's innately human to organize the world objectively and subjectively. It's as natural as telling time (objective) and liking chocolate (subjective). And as our daily lives increasingly rely on the Internet, it's clear that today's applications don't understand our subjectivity—not like we do. In the next sections, we'll look at how today's most popular tools—search engines, social networks, and recommendation algorithms—fundamentally aren't designed to manage the complexity of human subjectivity. We'll discuss why they will continue to overload us with content and prevent our products and content from getting discovered.

We'll also look at the solution. Millions of people are subjectively organizing content online in a process called curation—and it's growing at a scale not seen since the rise of Facebook. We'll investigate how curation is poised to cure the world from content overload and why you can't afford to be left behind. And if you think that discovering things in a better way won't affect you, then you need a history lesson: innovations in information retrieval and content discovery have led to the rise and fall of multibillion dollar companies such as Yahoo, Google, MySpace, Amazon, Facebook, and Twitter and along the way have fundamentally altered the way we make, buy, and sell everything. By the end of Part I, we'll have covered what content overload is, why some of today's largest technology companies haven't solved it yet, and how to position your business, blog, and YouTube videos for the coming curation age. To get there, we'll need to start where it all began: Web 1.0.

CHAPTER ONE

Web 1.0

The World's Biggest Card Catalog

In the early days of the web, the Internet was a massive bag of words. There were so many pages that we invented the world's biggest "card catalogs" to index them and called them "search engines." They had such names as AltaVista, Dogpile, Lycos, HotBot, Excite, MetaCrawler, Go.com, and Webcrawler and would search web pages for their titles, descriptions, and keywords. In 1997 Infoseek had 1.5 million pages of indexed text, AltaVista had 30 million, Excite had 50 million, and HotBot had 54 million.[1] Yahoo had human researchers, and if a search didn't match a researched category, they'd punt the query over to AltaVista for more automated results. And for a while, these search engines were useful.

That is, until Google arrived and blew off the hinges. Google's results were so much better that everyone started using its search engine and made Google one of the world's largest companies. Why was Google so much better? Was it because by the end of 1998, the company had an index of about 60 million pages and edged out the competition by size?[2] Or did Google have a secret sauce?

Google Leveraged Subjectivity

Google was better because its founders, Larry Page and Sergey Brin, moved beyond the idea of keyword search and figured out how to sort good from bad content. They did this by holding a sort of worldwide vote for the best websites and made the winners the top results on Google Search.

But Page and Brin didn't use surveys to hold this vote. Instead, they developed an algorithm called PageRank, which determines a web page to be good

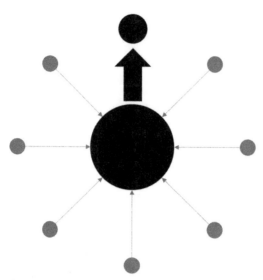

Figure 1.1   When many people vote for something, it's considered good. When the person behind the good thing votes for something, it's considered good too.

when it has a large quantity of inbound links or a few important inbound links (Figure 1.1). Think of it in terms of a lecture hall at Oxford University: The professor stands onstage and asks everyone to point to the smartest person in the room. It's likely that many students will point back to the professor; in that case, the professor receives a large number of votes and is judged as good. This is intuitive. But what does it mean when the professor points to someone?

If the professor points to a student, then even though the student receives just one vote, the student will also be judged as good because the student's endorsement came from a good source.

As Google saw them, links on the Internet were just like these classroom votes. Page and Brin believed that people link to content when it's worthy of attention, and like the Oxford professor pointing to the smartest student, some links are more important than others. By understanding that links are votes, Google tapped into the millions of subjective human evaluations of good content.

And Google Search was just better—it was more human. It makes sense that it would be better: it got the world to identify good content for users. So, when you searched for "baby strollers" you'd get a likable resource on the topic rather than a page that some spammer filled with the keywords "stroller" 1,000 times.

But if Google Search is so great, why didn't it fix everything?

The Content Changed

One reason we're overloaded with content is that the content changed. Back when the Internet was just a bag of words, it was supereasy to use Google Search to find what you needed; you were using words to find words. You want to know about trees? Search for articles with "trees" in it. Perfect.

But since Google launched in 1997, people worldwide came online and brought everything they had with them. This means that the activities of societies, cultures, and economies and all their associated imagery, videos, music, products, communication, news, commerce, and social media became searchable. A 2016 report by the United Nations indicated that 47 percent of the world's people now use the Internet, an increase from 2015 when the figure was 43 percent,[3] and that only about 50 percent of websites are in English.[4] In 2016, a full 73 percent of all Internet traffic was used to deliver video.[5] This is a tectonic transformation from the bag-of-words Internet; what we have today is an everything-in-the-world Internet.

And all the things humans make that aren't text-based—such as videos, music, pictures, and products—don't benefit equally from keyword search. In particular, the more aesthetic and subjective content becomes, the less it benefits from keywords. It's like Elvis Costello always said, "Writing about music is like dancing about architecture—it's a really stupid thing to want to do."[6] For example, how much do you like the song I just made up, "Under the Midnight Moon," by the artist I just made up, Kelly Stevens? I think it's great. It's superfun. I like cooking to it.

And that's exactly the point: you have no idea what kind of music I like to cook to. Is it hard rock? calypso? Is it any good? You can't tell by reading about it, just like reading "beautiful dresses here!" or "wonderful vacation destinations" doesn't help you know if you will think that the dresses are beautiful or the vacations are wonderful. In the land of subjectivity, words can mean many things and especially nothing at all.

But it wasn't just the content that changed; our expectations changed too.

We Changed

Another reason we still experience content overload is our heightened expectations. We have new desires to discover wonderful TV shows, products, art, music, videos, and content that delights us. We don't just want to search for stuff anymore—that would require us to know *exactly* what we want at all times. We want things to come to us. We want to discover great songs without knowing which bands recorded them. We want to discover quirky and beautiful terrarium bookshelves on Etsy without knowing the shop's name.

We want to find fantastic clothes outside the confines of a handful of mall shops. With everything "out there," it feels like an amazing discovery should be around every digital corner. And it does happen—some of the time. But in general, it's just too much work. And most of the time, setting out to discover something is an overwhelming experience. We want amazing discovery experiences without the exasperation of searching and sifting through everything all the time.

In 2016, Google was aware of over 130 trillion web pages on the Internet.[7] That's over 2 million times larger than the 60 million web pages it had available when it launched in 1998. Back in the late 1990s, a search engine would claim to be better because it offered more available pages. Does this mean that the Google of today is 2 million times better than it was before? Certainly, it shifts expectations toward thinking that everything that can be known must be out there. Any question you want answered and any video, or thing you'd like to purchase must be somewhere in those trillions of web pages. But given the possibility of finding it, does this mean we're happier than ever, always getting what we want?

Clearly, euphoria hasn't erupted the world over with parades in the street of everyone exclaiming how awesome it is to get exactly what they want all the time. In fact, just the opposite may be occurring; having more options available can in fact decrease well-being. Barry Schwartz, a psychologist at Swarthmore College, dubs this "the tyranny of choice" and observed the phenomenon across multiple studies.[8] For example, shoppers who have 6 jams to pick from are more likely to make a purchase than shoppers with 30 jams to consider. We're talking about a grocery store that really wants you to find the jam that's perfect for you with every kind of berry, non-GMO, gluten-free, and organic option and across multiple brands in glass jars or plastic-squeeze bottles. And yet that variety of choices, made to increase sales, makes people less likely to purchase jam at all.

In another example, a teacher provides students with the opportunity for extra credit. Students provided with 30 extra-credit topics are less likely to complete the assignment than those provided with 6 topics. And if that weren't enough, for those who do complete the assignment when there are 30 topics available, they do so with lower grades than those completing the assignment with only 6 topics available.

But maybe we only see the tyranny of choice when the decisions are low-stakes, such as buying jam or earning extra credit. Adults in the workplace dealing with their money would be less susceptible, right? Not at all. When employers offer more 401(k) investment options, employees become less likely to invest at all even when the company matches their contributions. That's literally saying no to free money, because the increase in the number of options make people feel that they can't decide at all.

Schwartz offers several possible reasons for why satisfaction drops amid increased choices. One is that there is the increased burden of gathering information (such as the 1,000 baby strollers that we can't sort by the ones we like most). More options mean that evaluating and sorting them right can be harder or impossible. Another possibility is that the knowledge of so many choices increases the likelihood of regretting the decision made. I mean, what if you evaluate 10,000 options for shoes, but the 10,001st option turns out to be the best choice? The prospect of missing out on this perfect shoe in turn leads to anticipating regretting the decision before even making it, resulting in the decision itself being even harder to make. Simultaneously, the presence of all these options leads to increased expectations that the perfect shoe must be out there, making what could be a great shoe seem relatively unappealing compared to the perfect as-yet-to-be shoe. And if you overcome the anticipated regret and then end up regretting a choice that doesn't live up to expectations, you only have yourself to blame. The perfect choice was out there, had you only found it.

Heightened expectations of finding what we want most demonstrates the cracks in our best search engines. Interestingly, the answer to the problem looks a lot more like the store manager preselecting six choice jams rather than having every jam in the world at your fingertips every time you want to make a peanut butter and jelly sandwich. And the difference between the two can be boiled down to the difference between push and pull.

Push versus Pull

As a retrieval tool, search pulls from the Internet whatever you type in; it's really good at that. With discovery, however, you don't have the keywords to type in; if you did, you would've just retrieved whatever it is you wanted in the first place (Figure 1.2). Like our store manager selecting only six jars of jam, discovery works best when new content is delivered, or pushed toward you. Some of the most popular implementations of the push model are Facebook's newsfeed, Instagram's photo feed, and Twitter's feed of tweets. After you make friends or follow people, the content just comes your way.

Now, this is not to say that discovery is passive; on the contrary, discovery often requires proactivity and the desire to try to evaluate new things. People with high appetites for discovery can evaluate lots of things that they don't particularly enjoy. And this is not to say that search can't do discovery, especially when researching new facts and information. But search and discovery benefit differently from push and pull experiences. By design, search's strength as a pull experience leaves it weak at discovery and push experiences.

Figure 1.2

Discovery Fail

With all that said, Google is not the perfect solution it once was. It's still useful, just not for everything. To summarize search's strengths and weaknesses, we can use a report card grading format. This report card takes what search is explicitly designed to do—retrieval—and measures it against its performance on what we end up using it for as well: discovery. The report card also looks at retrieval and discovery across the two relevant-use cases, including the desire for objective content, such as facts and information, and subjective content, such as songs, fiction, and anything that has to do with taste. So, it will retrieve four grades: grades for the retrieval of objective and subjective content, and grades for the discovery of objective and subjective content. The goal of the report card is to tease out what search does well (because it does a lot of things really well) while also calling out the places where it struggles (such as discovery). Let's see the results!

Retrieval of Objective and Subjective Content: A+

Search is fantastic if you know exactly what you want to retrieve. Search for "Polish kielbasa," and you'll get a kielbasa vendor. Search for "Tums," and you get Tums. It's as basic as it gets.

If you want subjective content such as songs, books, or art, as long as you know their names, it's all good; search retrieves them as well. You can retrieve the song to stream, get information about the band, find out when they're on tour, or look up their lyrics; it's all available.

Objective Discovery: B−

Search struggles when you want to discover stuff. If you want a cloud of information about a topic so you can explore in whatever direction you choose, then search isn't so bad. You want kielbasa recipes, history of kielbasa, secrets to how kielbasa is made, or how to become a vegetarian? They're all in the cloud of results for "kielbasa," each providing some relevance to the query provided. You still have to sift through them, but at least search got you in the ballpark.

Subjective Discovery: F

Search fails at discovering subjective content that doesn't match what is in the given query. It's like typing "clothes I want" into Google Search and expecting it to actually show you clothes you like: it just can't do that. Instead, you would get links to pages that mention the words "clothes," "I," and "want" not necessarily in that order. Pretty meaningless when taken as is.

Okay, so search is imperfect. But what's next?

For that, we keep following the path of technological innovation in subjectivity. And sadly, we have to leave Google behind.

This is shocking to me. How is it that Google didn't continue to innovate with subjectivity and create tools that embrace our humanity? After all, Google started out with this brilliant idea: let's design an algorithm to measure subjectivity on the web and make search better. Amazing. To that end, Google Search succeeded. It changed the world.

But now Google has become the company of mechanization, efficiency, and moon shots such as the privacy-invading Google Glass to self-driving cars. Maybe, though, we shouldn't be surprised. Despite its once touted "don't be evil" tagline, it is notable that Google's profits benefit from the status quo in search. Like General Motors shuttering electric car technology to protect sales of the once incredibly profitable Hummer, innovating your own products out of existence is not what big business tends to do.

And Google is big business. When you follow the money, you find that Google Search isn't just the dominant search engine; it's the goose that laid the golden egg: AdWords, otherwise known as Google's keyword-advertising cum money-printing machine. A shocking 90 percent of Google's revenue comes from AdWords keyword advertising: not Gmail, not Maps, not Google+, not Android, not Chrome, not self-driving cars, not drones, and not search itself, just advertising.[9] The free products that millions love arguably exist only to make sure we keep clicking on ads.

And companies such as Proctor & Gamble, General Mills, and Warner Brothers foot the bill for all our free fun, because they and millions of businesses like them buy ads that appear when we search with their sponsored keywords, whether they are subjective or not: "best smelling soap," "healthy kid's cereal," and "date-night movies" are typical search queries for which people will click on ads, but the ads are for content that is actually deeply subjective in nature.

Can you believe it? One of the most profitable advertising models in history relies on the fact that people continue to use Google for subjective discovery even though it's horrible at it (that's the section we just graded a big fat F). In fact, it's possible that Google makes the most money on subjective searches because it's so bad at them. When search is our primary discovery tool, we have to click on irrelevant ad after irrelevant ad, struggling in vain to find the baby stroller we like while depleting the advertising budgets of small business after small business. We leave empty-handed because our searches proved fruitless, while Google fattens its pockets because of all the ads clicked. But we continue to waste our time and advertising dollars for the same reason we wasted our time and money with Web 1.0 search engines such as AltaVista, Lycos, and Webcrawler: it's the best we've got right now.

So, it worked. Google's subjective search algorithm allowed the company to make the most powerful advertising machine on the Internet.

But an opportunity as big as making the web more human wouldn't stay untapped for long. While Google sat on its hands, others—namely social networks—came along and picked up the subjectivity trail.

CHAPTER TWO

Web 2.0

The Social Web

Web 2.0 is the social web, and Facebook established it more successfully than anyone else. Facebook was the first website to grow to 1 billion users and continues to grow in a seemingly inevitable march toward total global connectivity. In 2017 Facebook had a total of 2 billion users.[1] Keep in mind, there are around 7 billion people on the planet.[2]

Facebook is a social utility that helps people keep in touch with their friends, share updates and photos, and coordinate events; the platform makes it easier to communicate and share information in ways that used to be done in person, on the phone, or over e-mail or maybe hadn't happened before.

Much of Facebook's hype, however, is based in the idea that by knowing our identity, friends, conversations, and likes, Facebook will be able to beat Google. This sentiment was captured as early as 2008 when *Time* magazine wrote that "All these things you 'share' help connect you to your friends, but more importantly, they connect you to advertisers."[3] CNN went as far as to report two years later that "Facebook won the web" and that "links between Web pages are no longer the most abundant source of relevant recommendations. . . . The data gleaned from thousands of Facebook Like buttons around the web could make for an ad network that rivals Google's AdSense."[4]

"Could" turned out to be the critical word, however, because Facebook has yet to develop a search or advertising model that rivals Google, let alone beats it. Despite Google's weaknesses, the company remains more established today than ever before. Why is this? Why hasn't Facebook and the social web delivered a content discovery revolution?

Identity Is Complicated

Part of the reason Facebook hasn't lived up to its own hype is that we tend to primarily friend people we go to school with, work with, or live near. It's a social psychology phenomenon called propinquity that refers to people's tendency to befriend people who are in close proximity, such as in our neighborhoods, offices, or local cafés. This can be contrasted with where we are subjectively in our own heads. For example, you may objectively be sitting in your car driving to work, but subjectively, in your own head, you're riding a unicorn, sailing through the skies on your way to the gumdrop king's harvest festival. Or perhaps more typically, you're just enjoying a podcast. Out of the 50 cars in queue to pay a toll, all of them are objectively in the toll line, but the people inside the cars are subjectively they're listening to audiobooks, daydreaming, or talking on the phone.

While propinquity dominates the way most people actually make friends (after all, if they aren't nearby, how are we meeting them in the first place?), many people may think that they make friends based on their subjectivity. But while someone may have made a lot of like-minded friends in her or his community painting class, it's important to remember that the predominant reason that group came together is by living in the same town; the subjective interest in painting came second.

As a result, despite the potential to connect with anyone in the world, the average person on Facebook has only 190 friends.[5] And psychology professor Robin Dunbar found that among that group, only around 4 to 15 are considered friends you could rely on in a time of hardship.[6] The practical, physical, objective realities of meeting people and maintaining those relationships strongly determine your social network, not the subjective criteria.

It also means that the content you're discovering on social networks is largely based on the people you've been around. And while it's great to connect with some like-minded painters in your town, that's a small guarantee that they like the same kind of art that you do.

Connecting to people we know fits with Facebook's self-described role as a "social utility." Facebook is useful for sending messages to, sharing photos with, and organizing events with people we know. But as a means to discover new content, the people we know have many limitations. One limitation is that social media lacks focus.

Social Media's Lack of Focus

People have a fairly limited set of objective attributes, such as street address, employer, alma mater, family members, etc. But these objective attributes are dwarfed in magnitude by our subjective complexities. What are your views on art? What outfits do you like to wear? What are your favorite

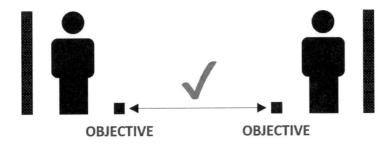

Figure 2.1 Friendship connections based on objective criteria, like someone's classmates, often saddle people with unintended subjective content (like political rants).

meals? Any of these questions could have 1,000 components, and there are thousands of these questions.

But when we friend someone based on where they live or work (which happens most of the time), we're then saddled with that person's subjectivity as well (Figure 2.1). While I might have friended someone because we're in the same history class, I now hear about his salami sandwich at lunch, the video games he's playing, or the articles he's liking. I'm too exposed to his subjectivity!

Now, that isn't always a bad thing, especially if your goal is to invest in people because of who they are. Uncle James isn't so bad, even if he only posts political rants. But if your goal is to discover new content for you, direct exposure to someone else's subjectivity can yield a lot of spam-like content. It's too unfocused. But a lack of focus is what we've come to expect from discovering content along objective, social ties.

Connecting to the people we know hurts discovery for another reason too, and it has to do with the small number of people we can actually meet, friend, and get to know.

Social Media Lacks Scope

Connecting to the people we know also hurts discovery because it limits the scope of our results. While there are over 7 billion people in the world, the average Facebook user receives updates from, again, only 190 of them. Remember that Google's key innovation, PageRank, leveraged the subjectivity of everyone on the Internet via the links they leave behind. Social networking—and the updates from your handful of friends—misses most objective and subjective information (Figure 2.2). It's like social networks have got us panning for gold with Dixie Cups when what we crave is mining equipment.

In addition to the limited number of sources, the order in which their updates appear is further shaped by hundreds of signals, many of which fall into one of four buckets.[7] The first is that Facebook considers who posted it and that person's relation to you. So, if you've interacted with this person's posts in the past, Facebook takes a guess that you'll likely want to interact with the person's posts again in the future. Interactions include liking or commenting on the person's posts, visiting the person's profile, and lingering over the person's posts (pretty much anything you could imagine to track, Facebook is likely tracking). Even if you're clicking on the post because it looks weird or awful, Facebook considers that kind of engagement the same as if you think a post is beautiful and edifying. After all, you did tap on it.

How other people engage with the post is another factor. If the first few people interact with it in some way, it's more likely to be prioritized and shown to more and more people afterward. If very few people interact with it, then it's destined to remain in obscurity. This has the potential to create an effect whereby the most active of your Facebook friends determine the content you'll likely to see from any of your friends. Because they're most active, they consistently see newly posted content first, becoming the litmus

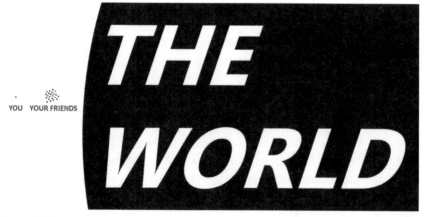

YOU   YOUR FRIENDS

Figure 2.2

test of engagement for their other friends. So, for example, if your most active friend on Facebook loves gossip and celebrities, then it's unlikely that this friend will respond to the economic and science articles that another one of your friend's post. And since those science articles were measured as "unengaging" by your "friends," you'll never see them. But it's likely that the gossip and celebrity news content will get a bump. And maybe you are interested in that. But what about your other friends and interests?

There are other criteria as well. For example, if you never watch videos but gaze at pictures, Facebook will likely tilt more pictures and fewer videos your way. Recency of a post matters too, though it's balanced with a popular post that you may not have seen and will be shown when you log back in after a week away.

Overall, the scope of social media is significantly limited. In the next section, we'll see how this is made more problematic by social ties lacking the ability to focus in on quality content as well.

Social Isn't a Great Signal

> [E]ven in a world of relatively few highly successful bestsellers, lists of favorites tend to be rather different, even between friends.
>
> Lada Adamic, research scientist and manager at Facebook

People love listing their favorite books on Facebook. A few years ago, a meme developed around this whereby people asked their friends to "list 10 books that have stayed with you in some way."[8] It became a large enough phenomenon that two data scientists at Facebook, Lada Adamic and Pinkesh Patel, decided to study it. Their goal was to better understand people and their lists of books.

Adamic and Patel started by building a data set of the favorite books that users posted by searching status updates for the keywords "10 books" or "ten books" over a two-week period. From this search, Adamic and Patel found and selected 130,000 top 10 book-related status updates for their study. After adding up the most popular books, they found that the most popular was *Harry Potter* (no surprises there), appearing on over 21 percent of lists. Next came *To Kill a Mockingbird* (14 percent), *The Lord of the Rings* (13 percent), *The Hobbit* (7 percent), and *Pride and Prejudice* (7 percent), rounding out the top 5 (Table 2.1).

As Adamic and Patel dug deeper into the results, they noticed something else; people tagged their friends at the bottom of their top 10 lists. For context, when friends tag each other on Facebook, they are explicitly notified that someone noted them in a message. And as is often the case with memes, there's a call to action to the other person (in this case, list your 10 favorite books). With friendship connections explicitly called out across people's lists

Table 2.1   Top 20 most popular books listed in a meme on Facebook

Percent of Lists Containing the Book	Title
21.08%	*Harry Potter* series, J.K. Rowling
14.48%	*To Kill a Mockingbird*, Harper Lee
13.86%	*The Lord of the Rings*, J. R. R. Tolkien
7.48%	*The Hobbit*, J. R. R. Tolkien
7.28%	*Pride and Prejudice*, Jane Austen
7.21%	*The Holy Bible*
5.97%	*The Hitchhiker's Guide to the Galaxy*, Douglas Adams
5.82%	The Hunger Games Trilogy, Suzanne Collins
5.70%	*The Catcher in the Rye*, J. D. Salinger
5.63%	*The Chronicles of Narnia*, C. S. Lewis
5.61%	*The Great Gatsby*, F. Scott Fitzgerald
5.37%	*1984*, George Orwell
5.26%	*Little Women*, Louisa May Alcott
5.23%	*Jane Eyre*, Charlotte Bronte
5.11%	*The Stand*, Stephen King
4.95%	*Gone with the Wind*, Margaret Mitchell
4.38%	*A Wrinkle in Time*, Madeleine L'Engle
4.27%	*The Handmaid's Tale*, Margaret Atwood
4.05%	*The Lion, the Witch, and the Wardrobe*, C. S. Lewis
4.01%	*The Alchemist*, Paulo Coelho

Source: Lada Adamic, "Books That Have Stayed with Us."

of books, it became possible for Adamic and Patel to ask the question "Do friends tend to like the same books?"

Surprisingly, the answer as it turns out is "no"; friends do not tend to like the same books—not in the least. The average friend shared 0.4 books. In other words, only every other pair of friends had one book in common. And this is true despite the fact that 21 percent of all lists contain *Harry Potter*!

One possible reason for the low book similarity among friends could be friends seeking to be unique in their answers. But even if this force toward differentiation exists among friends, the data shows that friends still have more in common than strangers: random people had 0.1 books in common on average. So, friends do have more in common than strangers—but not by much.

Bringing this back to the problem of discovery, the low similarity among friends refutes the once trumpeted belief that friendship connections create great recommendations. In fact, Facebook used to prominently declare that social connections would be a "cure-all" for discovery. When Facebook went public in 2012, the company wrote in its S-1 (the form that companies submit to the Securities and Exchange Commission before going public) that "We believe that the recommendations of friends have a powerful influence on consumer interest and purchase decisions."[9] At that time, it was extremely fashionable—practically common wisdom—to declare (sight unseen) that social recommendations would solve the problem of discovery.

The logic went like this: the best recommendations come from people you trust, and you trust your friends the most. And there is truth to this, especially if you need to discover something objective, such as a car mechanic who won't gouge you. That's a great question to ask your friends. Even if you don't have similar tastes, you both objectively don't want to get hustled.

But it's also half false, which we looked at earlier. Social media lacks the scope necessary to draw in a diversity of options as well as the focus necessary to match those options with one's subjective tastes. This creates a situation whereby you can receive a crippling number of recommendations that, ironically, lack a diversity of perspectives in addition to misaligning with your tastes.

During peak social media (around 2010–2012) when "everyone" believed that social media would solve discovery, some software developer colleagues of mine referred to the phenomenon as "socialitis." They found that Internet companies en masse wanted to jump onto the social networking train and give their users profiles and the ability to friend each other. And it didn't matter what you were selling. Fishing supplies? Your friends would help you buy more bait. Clothing? It should work even better! I mean, OMG, shopping with friends—online! There were even start-ups such as Ning that offered white-label social networks that anyone could start. For example, want to start a social network dedicated to the people in your apartment complex or to your corgi obsession? Ning has you covered!

Few socialitis integrations were more hotly anticipated and hyped as "game-changing" than those with music services that would let you discover music with friends. The culmination of this dream of "perfect music discovery with friends" was realized with the integration of Spotify with Facebook, a fusion of the world's largest free music-streaming service with the world's largest social network. While announcing the partnership, the founder of Spotify, Daniel Ek, called music "one of the most social things there is. . . . This integration with Facebook will help everyone to discover more free music than ever before."[10] The tech blog ReadWrite covered the partnership, writing at the beginning that you could "get personal recommendations by sending music you play to Facebook's Open Graph."[11]

But less than two months later a reversal came, and the same ReadWrite contributor wrote the follow-up piece, "Why I Shut Off Facebook's Spotify

Integration," noting that social networking is useful when his friends practice "curated, intentional sharing" but that "automated sharing is not very useful." He noted that "seeing a constant flow of songs in the news ticker is at best irrelevant and at worst annoying . . . most people don't care or need to know about every single song you listen to." Techdirt went further, saying "Why can't Spotify just be upfront and honest and say, 'spam all your friends on Facebook with what you're playing'?"[12] Worse still, the terrible spam-like recommendations started to be perceived as a breach of trust: "If these companies can't even get the basics right concerning how I can share my info, I'm going to have to look elsewhere. It's amazing how quickly a company can destroy a ton of goodwill." A year later the Spotify CEO owned up to the catastrophe, saying "social has always been a very big part of what we do at Spotify. But finding people who can introduce you to music you care about has been hard."[13] He wrote that it is "journalists, trendsetters, and artists . . . not just your friends, but really anyone on the music graph" who is effective at recommending music.

Social Struggles

While Facebook is incredibly useful for communication, the lack of subjective focus (too many political rants, Uncle James!) and lack of scope (why is there nothing I like here?) cripple it as a source of discovery. Applying the scorecard to social, we can assess grades across what social is explicitly designed for, such as objective communication (e.g., "we're meeting at 9:30 p.m.!") and subjective communication ("you're the cutest evah!"), and what social also ends up being used for, such as objective discovery (e.g., the recategorizing of Pluto as a dwarf planet) and subjective discovery (e.g., "OMG this song is so good!"). If social networks were to receive a report card, it might look something like the following.

Objective and Subjective Communication: A+

For communication, social networking is useful and relevant. Want to message a friend? Done. Want to share vacation photos with the family? Easy. People want to communicate with the people they know, and Web 2.0 sites such as Facebook are great solutions.

Objective Discovery: B

Social isn't the best at helping you discover stuff, but it isn't the worst either. If you want to join a group about kite building, you can do that on Facebook, on a forum, or on many social websites. If you're interested in discussing articles your friends are sharing, Facebook makes that easy as well. Social tools are one of many ways to discover objective content. In fact, in 2017 around two-thirds of Americans report that they got at least some of their news from social media, and this includes over half of Americans ages 50 and older (with 78 percent of those under age 50).[14] Clearly, for certain kinds of content, social does all right.

But in the end, social loses its grip on objective discovery too. For example, if it wanted to be better at objective discovery, it would need to look a lot more like Yelp. Yelp leverages the wisdom of the crowds (not just your friends) to evaluate all the restaurants and car repair shops. You don't need to like sushi for Yelp to help you find sushi places where the fish is fresh, the prices are reasonable, and the dining room is suitable for groups. Yelp leapfrogs social for objective discovery because it has scope (everyone reviewing everything) and doesn't try to provide the focus necessary for subjective discovery; it only does objective discovery and does it well.

Subjective Discovery: D

Facebook struggles with subjective discovery for the same reasons that it excels at communication: we often connect to people we know. And just because you want to communicate with your coworkers and classmates, this doesn't mean that you want to hear their political rants, teeny-bopper proclivities, or favorite 50 *Shades of Gray* quotes.

Despite Facebook's lack of focus and its limited scope, we do sometimes discover great content from our friends; it just doesn't happen as often or as easily as we might want.

But the trail of subjectivity doesn't stop with friending. There is another popular way to connect socially, and it's called "following." Whereas friending excels at communication, following excels at retrieving broadcasts from people you don't know. Let's look at how following and the company that captured it most successfully, Twitter, changed the discovery equation.

Following

Following people is a fundamental part of the social web, and Twitter pioneered it more successfully than any other company. The invention of following was by all accounts an accident—Twitter founders Evan Williams, Jack Dorsey, and Biz Stone say that they didn't set out to revolutionize communication. Rather, they developed Twitter as a side project within their now defunct media directory start-up Odeo, and to everyone's surprise, it took on a life of its own. When Twitter launched, its founders described it as "ice cream: not that useful, but a fun thing."[15] It's a laughable description today considering the pressure that Twitter puts on the news media industry, the platform it gave to President Donald Trump, the multiple hundred million–user juggernaut it became, and its market cap in the tens of billions of dollars.

At the time, though, it wasn't clear that the ability to follow others—and read whatever crossed their mind—was anything but a waste of time. In 2009 only a few years after Twitter's launch, Maureen Dowd at the *New York Times* commented that she "would rather be tied up to stakes in the Kalahari Desert, have honey poured over me and red ants eat out my eyes than open a Twitter account."[16] Today, however, she tweets from the account @maureendowd with over 667,000 followers.

On Twitter, people follow each other and receive short 120-character messages called "tweets." Following someone is like subscribing to a newsletter: you receive messages from others but they don't receive anything from you— unless they follow you back. Their tweets show up in your "feed" as soon as they're sent, providing a window into what's happening "right now." Twitter's website describes the platform as "an easy way to discover the latest news related to subjects you care about."[17] It's an accurate description, because people do tend to use the short, public, real-time, nonfriendship-based following relationships to share news-like updates.

Twitter rose in popularity after Facebook, because following offers two things that friending does not. First, you can follow as many people as you want, and no one can stop you. This addresses the small scope on Facebook, because if you wanted to, you could follow millions of people (Facebook has since added the ability to follow).

Second, because people primarily use Twitter to share news, tweets tend to follow a theme. This stands in stark contrast to the general communication about everything and anything on Facebook.

With its wide scope of thematically organized information, it's no surprise that Twitter became a major social media platform. In fact, it seems that Twitter solved the two major content discovery problems on Facebook— scope and focus. But does this that mean Twitter is the solution to content overload? As anyone who has used Twitter knows, not even close.

In April 2014 the *Wall Street Journal* wrote that "Wall Street is coming to grips with the possibility that Twitter may remain a niche service, rather than become the next Facebook." The article points out the cold reality that "While Twitter has proven to be a powerful communications tool for celebrities, activists, marketers, and journalists, it hasn't caught on with mainstream users."[18] This evaluation has largely proven itself. In April 2014, Twitter's stock price was around $40. In the fourth quarter of 2017 it was around $18, more than a 50 percent decline with growth stagnant.

How can this be? How can a company that solves two of Facebook's major discovery problems remain niche?

Pick a Niche or Die

Part of the reason Twitter remains a niche service is that, in general, people are corralled into picking a niche in order to gain followers. You start to get this sense when you read Twitter's "help" page suggesting that new users shouldn't actually tweet: "Some people find it useful to contribute their own Tweets," says Twitter, "but the real magic of Twitter lies in absorbing real-time information."[19] It's not every day you hear a Web 2.0 company suggest that only some people should contribute to the service. But since the real magic of Twitter is found by only some people tweeting, Twitter suggests that new users "look for businesses you love, public service accounts, people you know, celebrities, or news sources you read." Pretty much, just follow someone you already know of.

The emphasis on niches continues in instructions on how to tweet: "Use Twitter to share unique information" is what Twitter tells businesses looking to market on Twitter.[20] *PC Magazine* chimes, in saying that people should "name your area of expertise or interest in your bio. If you want more Twitter followers . . . [y]ou need a theme."[21] The magazine recommends "tweet[ing] on topic 80 percent of the time . . . to deliver on the promise you've made in your profile." And it's sensible advice: if you want to be successful on Twitter—if you want to gain followers—it's smart to pick a niche (Figure 2.3).

Like reviewing past issues of *Wired* magazine before paying to subscribe, a niche enables prospective followers to review past tweets to decide if they want similar future tweets. If I see that the Food Network posts a lot of recipes, then I have confidence that the network won't start tweeting about penny stocks.

In contrast, for people who use Twitter as a general communication tool and tweet about anything and everything (as on Facebook), they create the same lack of focus that we experience on Facebook. As the *New York Times* observed, "To get real value out of the service, a user has to invest a lot of effort up front, be it deciding which accounts to follow or determining how

SUBJECTIVE   **SUBJECTIVE**

Figure 2.3   It's easier to follow someone with compatible subjective interests when they pick and stick to a niche.

to sift useful bits of information from the irrelevant chatter that can easily fill up each person's feed."[22]

Twitter doesn't want "irrelevant chatter"; people who want "useful bits of information" don't want it either. So, Twitter continues to recommend picking a niche. And in the distant future when everyone finds their niche and everyone finds the right people to follow, then we'll finally be in a position to discover the content we really want. Sounds like a good plan to fix content overload, right? It would be, except for two fatal flaws.

One-Dimensionality

Want to tweet about your job and personal life? Pick one. Want to tweet about your favorite music and movies? You need to pick one. Want to tweet about your favorite classical and electronic music? If you want a niche, you need to pick one. Want to tweet about your favorite 20th-century and 19th-century composers? You get the idea.

Sticking with a theme requires trade-offs. And most of the time, this comes at the cost of forgoing other interests (Figure 2.4). No matter how much the social media team at the Food Network might be interested in cars, poetry, or dubstep, they can't tweet about them without betraying their followers' trust. It doesn't matter how good the dubstep track is: if people are expecting blueberry tart recipes, a "killer" bass-drop from Skrillex won't be appreciated.

Like the Food Network, our own niches pigeonhole us, and we become forever stuck tweeting about our jobs or products—because if we have to pick one niche, we usually pick the most important one. And with everyone pigeonholed, engaging in never-ending water cooler talk, everyone loses out. By withholding our full array of interests, we create a poverty of interests to discover.

But it's not just the one-dimensionality that limits Twitter's usefulness; it's also its obsession with the "latest" and most "real-time" content.

OBJECTIVE   SUBJECTIVE

Figure 2.4 Niches encourage people to withhold their full array of interests.

The Feed Favors Speed

Twitter's second fatal flaw is also its primary strength: the real-time delivery of information. While real time is great for breaking news, if you want to discover content that stays relevant for more than a few minutes, the volume of information happening right now almost always swamps it.

The Twitter feed is like the world's largest peanut gallery commenting on current events. As the *Wall Street Journal* put it, "Given its fast-paced nature, Twitter's service can at times make users feel like they are alone in a crowded room."[23] And this feeling of disconnection happens despite the ability to follow anyone you want—even because of it.

It's very difficult to escape the feed's fire hose of updates. Consider that it could be you who, after painting the next *Mona Lisa* and tweeting your modern masterpiece to the world—whooosh!—gets buried by 1,000 photos of Cardi B vacationing, never to be seen again. Perhaps this is why the average user on Twitter, despite the ability to connect to anyone, only follows 102 people.[24]

Chamath Palihapitya joined Facebook in 2007 and became its vice president for user growth, responsible for coming up with strategies to gain and retain users. While speaking to a group of Stanford Graduate School of Business students (and having left Facebook), Palihapitiya said that "he feels 'tremendous guilt' about the company he helped make." He criticized the superficial, emotionally driven, "feed"-based ecosystem of news and content delivery, saying that "I think we have created tools that are ripping apart the social fabric of how society works." On the topic of feeds favoring speed, he said that "the short-term, dopamine-driven feedback loops we've created are destroying how society works, . . . hearts, likes, thumbs-up. . . . No civil discourse, no cooperation; misinformation, mistruth. . . . And it's not an American problem. . . . This is a global problem."[25]

The world of content is much broader and more diverse than the speed-obsessed feed can give justice. For example, it's not a coincidence that news content dominates on Twitter, with 63 percent of users saying that the platform serves as a source of news.[26] News is most relevant as soon as it's published and has an extremely short shelf life, with the next article eclipsing the prior one as a more accurate reflection of the ever-moving "right now."

Content is produced differently depending on what span of time it's meant to be relevant within (Figure 2.5). On the extremely short end of the spectrum we have tweets and text messages, often meant to be consumed one second and forgotten the next. At the other extreme we have world wonders such as the pyramids, architectural feats made to last for millennia and to be timeless.

Content exists in every place between as well. For example, the art of Leonardo Da Vinci has fascinated audiences for over 500 years, and the music of Beethoven has enthralled audiences for over 200 years. *Don Quixote* has remained on reading lists for over 400 years, first being published in 1605. And there are novels being written today that will be relevant for 100 years too. When Hollywood makes a blockbuster, I doubt that a studio

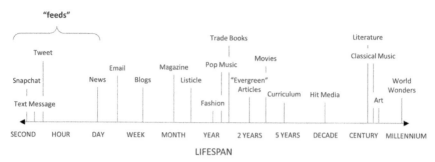

Figure 2.5 The lifespan of content can vary dramatically.

has hopes that it will be relevant for 100 years, but it does hope that it's the "most" relevant for at least the summer.

David Bawden and Lyn Robinson are academics with the Department of Information Science at the City University of London. They hypothesize that as we consume information at faster and faster speeds, our expectations toward that content changes as well. For example, they observe that social media tools enable quick, incremental changes to content, which enable more content to be published faster, and that in turn heightens consumer expectations of novelty (even if the novelty produced isn't very original). They write that "The nature of web 2.0 tools also promotes an information landscape based on shallow novelty. Because the tools allow, and encourage, rapid updating and posting of new material, there emerges an expectation of constant novelty. Because genuinely significant new material is as hard as ever to discover or produce, this expectation can be satisfied only by the re-using of existing material, by linking or re-packaging, or by the generation of shallow and ephemeral material."[27] They also observe that feeds themselves tend to reward "tiny" content and not "longform" content: "the nature of the tools themselves—consider RSS feeds and podcasts as examples—are well suited to 'soundbites' and 'microchunks' of decontextualised information. Naturally, these are easier and quicker to produce, and to assimilate, than more thoughtful and deeply researched material." Because the feed is just small pieces of content racing past each other, it actually encourages the production of more small content.

Disney is notably capable of avoiding the trap of short-term engagement; the studio understands that it's genuinely hard to to produce new films and do a tremendous job taking the relatively short life span of family entertainment and turning it into "evergreen" content that every family must watch every generation. Part of that strategy includes releasing its films for purchase in limited batches, thereby never saturating the market with an "always available" product that in turn will also become dated. Disney has proven that it is able to rerelease films over and over again, reminding audiences that

Table 2.2 *Bambi* box-office revenues

Year	Revenue	Inflation Adjusted Revenue	Multiple
1942	$3,000,000	$46,914,458	1.0x
1947	$2,200,000	$25,122,874	0.5x
1957	$6,000,000	$53,373,695	1.1x
1966	$9,000,000	$69,486,509	1.5x
1975	$20,000,000	$94,249,136	2.0x
1982	$23,000,000	$59,882,682	1.3x
1988	$39,047,150	$82,859,267	1.8x

Source: "*Bambi*—Lifetime Gross: $102,247,150," Boxoffice Mojo.

its timeless stories are only ever available for a limited time. The year 2017 marked the 75th anniversary of *Bambi* and its release on DVD—again. It's even possible to track *Bambi*'s box office rereleases going back to World War II. How many other film studios are able to rerelease their films for half a century? The box-office revenues in Table 2.2 are taken from Boxoffice Mojo and converted into 2017 inflation-adjusted dollars.[28]

Interestingly, we see that even though *Bambi* was released to the public every 6 to 10 years over a 46-year period, the revenues, including the inflation-adjusted revenues, were almost always higher than in the launch year.

Twitter and the feed are not made to construct timeless classics such as this. If Disney had allowed *Bambi* to only have its first theater release, the studio would have left nearly $385 million on the table. Indeed, the "following" model's inability to accommodate anything but the most ephemeral content comes at significant cost and, when it comes to discovery, causes it to falter.

Following Falters

While Twitter excels at broadcasting real-time news, it suffers from one-dimensionality and attention deficit disorder. For the following scorecard, we'll rate Twitter on what it's meant to be used for—a kind of communication/publication tool—and also in the way that it's used to discover content. If following were to receive a report card, it might look something like the following.

Objective and Subjective Communication: B

When used for communication purposes, the ability to "follow" someone is like a modern-day water cooler: you typically learn objective information about what others are doing and subjective information about how they're feeling. And while these updates can be timely, useful, and entertaining, they're also quickly forgotten.

Objective Discovery: B+

When used to discover objective content, following people is like being a groupie. When Maroon 5 performs at the MTV Video Music Award ceremony, their followers get to see pictures from backstage. Fans of the Food Network get to feel like they're in the studio kitchen as they discover the perfect chicken marinade. Followers of VentureBeat get to feel like they're in the newsroom as they learn about Apple's acquisition of Beats. Twitter enables you to pick your own sources, and while there are many places to get the news, Twitter offers many unique direct perspectives from the sources themselves.

Subjective Discovery: D+

Twitter struggles with subjective discovery for the same reasons that it's great at real-time news. First, Twitter traffics in bit-size ephemera—if you want to discover something that's relevant for more than a day (max), you're out of luck. Second, it's almost impossible to gain followers without already being famous or, as is recommended, picking a niche. This has the unfortunate side effect of depriving Twitter of a rich variety of interests and depriving us of the ability to follow them. It's still possible to discover things you like especially quick-hit content such as blog posts or sketch art, but only despite its design, not because of it.

So, there you have it. Web 2.0 and its social innovations of friending and following have revolutionized communication and the way we discover information, but they haven't solved the problem of content overload (but we already knew that, didn't we?). So, where does the path of technological innovation in subjectivity lead us next?

For our final investigation, let's put the messy social world behind us and travel to the land of PhDs and scientists. Let's visit the "genius" algorithms that power our recommendation engines and see if machine learning experts can show us the light.

Recommendation Engines

We see them everywhere: "People who like this also like that." Amazon, Netflix, and YouTube all make such recommendations. They do it because the promise of algorithms is seductive: use data from millions to tailor recommendations for the individual. And there's precedent: Google's rise to dominance came out of an algorithm that measured the subjectivity of millions. The technology behind recommendation engines is extremely sophisticated, with some of the best minds in computer science and mathematics advancing the state of the art. And the results are useful, sometimes, but it's clear that "People who like this also like that" is far from solving the problem of content overload (I've yet to see a baby stroller on Amazon where by looking at what other people bought, I discovered the stroller I will like the most). In fact, online product discoverability is so weak that 79 percent of all impulse buys are still made in stores.[29]

It gets worse—much worse. Beyond not helping people find what they want, the recommendation engines, ironically, give people more of what they've already found. They're guilty of creating echo chambers of similar content and, when it comes to the news media, facilitates the transmission of fake news and conspiracy theories. Critics warn that these systems threaten democracy itself, pointing to election results such as those for Trump and social unrest around the world.

So why aren't advanced algorithms working? What's stopping Amazon's "people who bought this also bought that" algorithm from curing content overload? And why are these system implicated in spreading propaganda, creating social unrest, and acting unethically? Let's start with the elephant in the room and address how the design of these systems threatens democracy itself.

Recommendation Engines Lack Ethics

The Internet has always been a place for everyone—even the worst of us. And when recommendation engines take content generated by the worst of us, amplify it, and present it to everyone, you get severe unintended consequences for community, society, and democracy.

Evan Williams is an Internet publishing pioneer, having founded many of the most influential digital writing platforms including the blogging platform Blogger (acquired by Google), the suffocatingly omnipresent microblogging platform Twitter (now public with a market capitalization of about $26 billion), and, most recently, the long-form publishing platform Medium, which has raised $132 million in funding. Yet despite his success in shaping the Internet, Williams thinks that the Internet has become dysfunctional (including his creations): "I think the Internet is broken. . . . And it's a lot more obvious to a lot of people that it's broken."[30] How broken is it? Pretty broken, in his view; he says it's the worst of us pushed on the rest of us. As the *New York Times* describes it, "People are using Facebook to showcase suicides, beatings and murder, in real time. Twitter is a hive of trolling and abuse that it seems unable to stop. Fake news, whether created for ideology or profit, runs rampant. Four out of 10 adult Internet users said in a Pew survey that they had been harassed online. And that was before the presidential campaign heated up last year." Essentially, it's digital bedlam.

More and more digital experts are coming to the conclusion that much of the dysfunction is the unintended consequences of recommendation engines built primarily to maximize attention and advertising revenue, not decency. As it turns out, what captures most people's attention (the least common denominator) also has a dark side. As Williams puts it, the Internet rewards "extreme" content, regardless of its morality. He likens the phenomenon to rubbernecking on the highway, where everyone can't help but look at the carnage: "The trouble with the Internet . . . is that it rewards extremes. Say you're driving down the road and see a car crash. Of course you look. Everyone looks. The Internet interprets behavior like this to mean everyone is asking for car crashes, so it tries to supply them. Maybe it will be all car crashes, all the time. Twitter already feels like that."[31] Let that sink in; the cofounder of Twitter says that his creation feels like a car crash and that it creates incentives to make new "crashes," because clearly that's what everyone looks at.

With just a modicum of scrutiny, the design of the Internet looks quite naive. Much of its original architecture was made for information to flow freely, which is great when everyone is a good actor. But it falls flat on its face when bad actors arrive. As Williams remarks, "I thought once everybody could speak freely and exchange information and ideas, the world is automatically going to be a better place. . . . I was wrong about that. . . . The problem is that not everyone is going to be cool, because humans are humans. . . . There's a lock on our office door and our homes at night. The internet was started without the expectation that we'd have to do that online."[32] And most of the gatekeeping that controls flows of information (e.g., recommendation engines) is optimizing for attention, not quality or ethics per se. As Williams describes it, "Ad-driven systems can only reward attention. . . . They can't reward the right answer." Interestingly, Williams is bullish on curation, hypothesizing a solution that resembles the bookstore model, because rather than commissioning material, bookstores instead curate and sell it.

Renee DiResta is an ideas contributor for *Wired* and a Mozilla fellow on media, misinformation, and trust and is affiliated with the Berkman-Klein Center at Harvard and the Data Science Institute at Columbia University. She shares many of Williams's concerns about the Internet and with recommendation engines in particular. But beyond letting bad actors loose, she observes specifically that these systems drive social polarization both online and offline. She writes that "today, recommendation engines are perhaps the biggest threat to societal cohesion on the Internet—and, as a result, one of the biggest threats to societal cohesion in the offline world, too. The recommendation engines we engage with are broken in ways that have grave consequences: amplified conspiracy theories, gamified news, nonsense infiltrating mainstream discourse, misinformed voters. Recommendation engines have become The Great Polarizer."[33]

DiResta points out that recommendation tools, despite leveraging the subjective opinions and ratings from real people, are amoral; they're agnostic megaphones, amplifying lies and hate as easily as anything else. Observing the behavior of Pinterest's, Twitter's, and Facebook's recommendation systems in particular, she finds that "the Pinterest algorithms don't register a difference between suggesting duckie balloons and serving up extremist propaganda; the Twitter system doesn't recognize that it's encouraging people to follow additional extremist accounts, and Facebook's Groups engine doesn't understand why directing conspiracy theorists to new conspiracy communities is possibly a bad idea. The systems don't actually understand the content, they just return what they predict will keep us clicking."[34]

To DiResta, the design of recommendation systems comes down to "curatorial decisions." She asks if it's possible to make them more ethical especially as they become more pervasive. DiResta points out that "as the consequences of curatorial decisions grow more dire, we need to ask: Can we make the internet's recommendation engines more ethical? And if so, how? The need to rethink the ethics of recommendation engines is only growing more urgent as curatorial systems and AI [artificial intelligence] crop up in increasingly more sensitive places."[35]

YouTube's recommendation system isn't immune to ethical dilemmas either. Zeynep Tufekci is an associate professor at the School of Information and Library Science at the University of North Carolina and writes that regardless of which video you start with, YouTube's algorithm then ratchets up the intensity of inflammatory content. This means that if you start with a moderate opinion on an issue, YouTube next nudges you toward more extreme opinions. In Tufekci's experience, "It seems as if you are never 'hard core' enough for YouTube's recommendation algorithm. It promotes, recommends and disseminates videos in a manner that appears to constantly up the stakes. Given its billion or so users, YouTube may be one of the most powerful radicalizing instruments of the 21st century."[36] She sees this radicalization as a form of manipulation, since YouTube, fueled by a desire for profit, designs ways to convert our attention into advertising dollars. Tufekci says that "What we are witnessing is the computational exploitation of a natural human desire: to look 'behind the curtain,' to dig deeper into something that engages us. As we click and click, we are carried along by the exciting sensation of uncovering more secrets and deeper truths. YouTube leads viewers down a rabbit hole of extremism, while Google racks up the ad sales."

Most interestingly, she finds that Google and YouTube have in general shielded themselves from responsibility, pointing out that they're merely giving people what they want. After all, YouTube doesn't force people to search for, watch, and then keep watching its videos: "In effect, YouTube has created a restaurant that serves us increasingly sugary, fatty foods, loading up our plates as soon as we are finished with the last meal. Over time, our tastes adjust, and we seek even more sugary, fatty foods, which the restaurant dutifully provides. When confronted about this by the health department and concerned citizens, the restaurant managers reply that they are merely serving us what we want."[37]

On a more empowering note, Tufekci says that we don't have to be complacent with the status quo; YouTube doesn't have to be allowed to generate so much profit at society's expense. As she puts it, "This state of affairs is unacceptable but not inevitable. There is no reason to let a company make so much money while potentially helping to radicalize billions of people, reaping the financial benefits while asking society to bear so many of the costs."[38] And she's absolutely right. What all of these systems lack is the ability to leverage the judgment, morality, and ethics built into a curator's subjectivity. If recommendation systems learned how to work with curators instead of stripping them of their protective gatekeeping, we'd be in a much better position. Sadly, the most common recommendation technologies themselves work against this principal. There's another reason as well that keep recommendation engines from reaching their potential. It's called the "magic barrier," and even if the ethical issues were solved, it still holds the technology back.

The Magic Barrier

Collaborative filtering is one of the most common and highly developed recommendation techniques. On YouTube, for example, a collaborative filter can analyze everyone's thumbs-up and thumbs-down ratings to find videos that are often coliked. That way, when you're watching Katy Perry sing "Dark Horse," YouTube can suggest Perry's video *Roar* next. And it sort of works.

But after decades of study, researchers have made just incremental improvements to this kind of recommendation. Why? Because the magic barrier keeps it from working better.

The magic barrier is a mysterious boundary beyond which no collaborative filter can improve; it's as if an invisible wall blocks an ever-optimizing algorithm from achieving perfection. It's suspected to exist because people themselves are too inconsistent.[39] The thought is that if people rate videos with three stars when really they liked it at four stars, then the collaborative filter, no matter how good it is, will be inconsistent too. In other words, the math is fine; the problem is people.

But this theory hasn't stopped anyone from trying to make improvements. For example, one of the most publicized and closely watched events in collaborative filtering history was the Netflix Prize, launched in 2006, a $1 million reward to whoever could improve the accuracy of the Netflix recommendation algorithm by 10 percent.[40] A team composed of researchers from AT&T

Research, Yahoo Research, and several independent firms won it three years later.[41] After competing and collaborating with some of the most ambitious and brilliant computational minds, they won with a 10.06 percent improvement.

With the competition over, one Netflix engineer hypothesized that it took over three years to get a winner because the 10 percent goal was inadvertently too close to the magic barrier.[42] The winning team's solution supports this hypothesis: they blended 127 different algorithms together to squeeze out the last few points of improvement. Hardly a single aha moment.

While Netflix did cherry-pick a select few of those algorithms to use for itself,[43] the company didn't actually use the winning solution.[44] For starters, it was deemed too complicated for production.[45] But more importantly, it no longer worked. By 2009 Netflix had launched streaming video, and as it turns out, the Netflix Prize used data from the mail delivery system. The differences between snail mail and online streaming changed how people watch and rate videos and erased the winning team's hard-won 10 percent improvement. In effect, the hard-won gains snapped back as the magic barrier showed itself in full force.

And the magic barrier isn't the only problem with today's collaborative filters. There's a deeper riddle hidden in the ratings themselves.

The Least Common Denominator

There's probably truth to the idea that people inconsistently rate DVDs—but this reason feels insufficient. Am I to believe that I only sometimes dislike *Scary Movie 3*? I'd like to think that I and most other people know our own likes and dislikes. That the algorithm would work better if only the people weren't so faulty seems like a cop-out. Furthermore, some recommendation engines don't rely on ratings at all: beyond what you've rated, Amazon knows what you actually bought, but nonetheless, "Customers Who Bought This Item Also Bought" hits the magic barrier too. So, what's really causing the problem?

As it turns out, there's a cause that makes it seem like otherwise consistent people act randomly. Consider for a moment emptying everything in your home into a giant pile. In this pile we find your toothbrush on top of your TV next to an antique mirror that leans against a box of Cheerios. Could someone examining this pile see the deep, underlying patterns behind your tastes, perspectives, and preferences? Can we divine if you eat Cheerios for breakfast versus as a midnight snack? We may only agree that such a pile would look like the messiest house of all time. In fact, we might determine that this pile looks pretty senseless. But this pile of everything we own is similar to our piles of movie ratings on Netflix or the piles of products we bought on Amazon: one after another we buy, rate, and grow a massive, undifferentiated pile of stuff that, if you look at it all at once, is a complete mess.

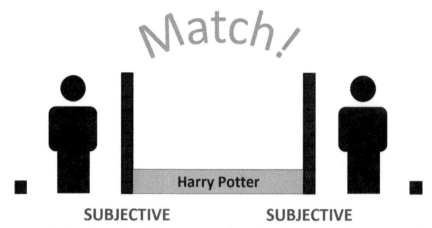

Figure 2.6 When algorithms process editorial-style ratings, the most significant trends often appeal to the lower common denominator.

And we task collaborative filters with determining our tastes from these messes. And you know what associations they find after comparing everyone's massively messy, undifferentiated piles of stuff? We all like *Harry Potter* (Figure 2.6). And for those who don't yet have a copy of *Harry Potter* in their giant mess of stuff, that will be the first recommendation because, as the data shows, most people have *Harry Potter* in their mess somewhere.

Now, that's not to say *Harry Potter* is a bad recommendation per se. But it is one that appeals to the lowest common denominator. And getting recommended what's popular over and over again gets old. In one Wharton study, it was found that collaborative filters "create a rich-get-richer effect for popular products"[46] due to recommending what people already know or could have easily found out.[47] Our unique interests and niche passions, regardless of how prominent they are in our lives, are by design lost among more statistically significant mainstream trends. The reality is that by the time algorithms go to work on our messy piles, the meaningful patterns have already become indecipherable, like a Buddhist monk who's already erased the image of his mandala. No matter how capable algorithms become at finding meaningful patterns, they will never succeed if the meaning is no longer there.

The Least Common Denominator Continues to Grow: The Case of YouTube

YouTube democratized video publishing for the world; for those with stars in their eyes, it truly became possible for anyone to upload a video and find their audience. But increasingly, the only way to make it on YouTube is to make it "big" or not at all, hollowing out the "middle-class" of creators. And it's becoming much harder to make it big.

"Making it" on YouTube looks like entering the top 3.5 percent of most viewed channels, which according to the *Washington Post* receive at least 1 million views per month and pull in $12,000 to $16,000 per year of advertising revenue (about $1,200 per month).[48] A study by Mathias Barlt, professor of applied sciences at Offenburg University in Germany, found that while successful people on YouTube continue to be successful, it has become a lot harder to become successful in the first place. For example, getting views at all is harder than ever; whereas the median number of views per video was 10,262 in 2006, 10 years later it plummeted to 89 views. At the same time, top channels continue to grow larger: the top 3 percent of channels dominated 90 percent of all views in 2016, whereas in 2006 it was only 64 percent. The *Washington Post* noticed that this phenomenon is not isolated to YouTube, observing that "what's happening on YouTube is occurring across the Web, where creators are finding that long odds of success in the online world are not so different from IRL (Internet-speak for 'in real life'). In fact, they might be worse." For example, the market research firm Nielsen found that 86 percent of all music streamed in 2017 was from only 1 percent of the songs, leaving the vast majority of bands out in the cold to "face the pressure of going viral or going home." To make matters more challenging for creators, YouTube is changing its policies to make establishing oneself on the platform even harder; before allowing a video to display an ad (and allowing the creator to receive compensation for her or his work), the company is now requiring the creator's channel to have at least 1,000 subscribers and 4,000 hours of watch time over the past 12 months; this would require a five-minute video to be viewed 48,000 times per month (remember, the average video is only viewed 89 times in total). YouTube says that the change is "aimed at discouraging videos with objectionable or offensive content and that it would 'affect a significant number of channels.'" Regardless of the reason, this creates additional barriers to establishing a YouTube "middle class." And across these services we continue to see consolidation toward the least common denominator as a decreasing share of creators dominate an increasing share of the attention and rewards. While it's impossible to attribute this development entirely to algorithms, the "rich get richer" effect that they amplify is absolutely part of the problem.

Algorithms Hit a Wall

While collaborative filters use advanced algorithms, they're only sometimes useful. Not only do they run up against the magic barrier, but they also tend to recommend things that we already know or could have easily found out. If collaborative filters were to receive a report card, it might look something like the following.

Subjective Discovery: C—

Collaborative filters help us discover some things that we like, and so far these filters have received the highest score for subjective discovery on our list—and we'll take what we can get! But today's recommendation engines are far from becoming the "Google" for discovery. Beyond their documented limitations, they can be outright frustrating (e.g., stop recommending *Twilight*!), and as a result, few people visit "People Who Bought This Also Bought These" to discover something new. Worse still, it's found that they can have a radicalizing effect, pushing people toward ever more extreme content, because like a car crash, it's captivating to the least common denominator in many of us.

So, where does that leave us? Is there any hope to solving the problem of discovery?

Even though the Web 2.0 inventions of friending, following, and algorithmic recommendation produced high expectations and big disappointments, there exists another mechanism that's almost as old as humanity itself—and it has only recently started taking off online. In the next chapter we explore curation and explain how it's revolutionizing content discovery.

CHAPTER THREE

Dawn of the Curation Age

The Problem of Scope and Focus

There are billions of phones in the world, and with the right phone number, you can connect to any of them. You could say that the phone system answered our desire to communicate with anyone (huge scope) one call at a time (focus) (Figure 3.1). Many of our most celebrated organizational inventions accomplish similar feats. For example, the Dewey decimal system helps us find specific books among a huge selection. The postal system delivers letters to specific buildings among millions. And Google enables us to take a huge scope of web pages and focus on specific results.

Before you can focus, you have to have scope, and getting a wide scope can be difficult. Before you could dial anyone in the world, everyone in the world had to first have a phone. Before a card catalog could easily point you

Figure 3.1

to any book, you had to first have all the books in one place. For the postal service to do its delivery magic for anyone, you have to first have homes with addresses on them. And for Google to retrieve specific web pages for us, it first has to have knowledge of all the web pages. As scope broadens, the value of focus increases.

But for the things we like, such as music, books, movies, art, and fashion, is there a way to assess everything (have a huge scope) according to our own tastes (a subjective focus)? What would it look like? To dive into this topic, we need to address an even more fundamental question first: What is taste anyway?

Twin Pillars of Taste

Imagine a glass of red wine. A social drinker—who's never paid attention to his beverage—takes a sip and likes it. The same glass in the hands of a sommelier, however, transforms into a full-bodied cabernet sauvignon with hints of oak and cherry and, while he thinks that it overpowers the evening's hors d'oeuvres, it remains to him a standout choice among the 2009 cabernets.

The taste buds of our social drinker and sommelier are practically identical. The sensory stimulus sent from their taste buds to their brains is practically identical. It's their brain's interpretation of the sensory stimulus that's different. With thousands of differentiated wines in the sommelier's memory, he interprets the glass within a rich web of comparisons. The social drinker compares it to beer (Figure 3.2).

Our sommelier highlights the first element of taste: spotting differences. Ferdinand de Saussure pioneered this way of thinking in a field of study called semiotics (the study of "signs," or why things mean something) in which he defined a concept as "being what the others are not."[1] He realized

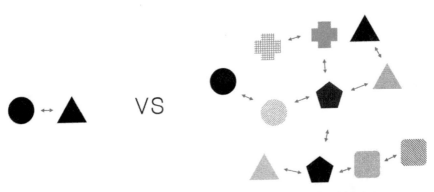

Figure 3.2 The twin pillars of taste are differentiation and subjectivity.

that for anything to mean something, we must first understand how it is different. This is one reason why when you first hear a foreign language, the words incomprehensibly blur together (it all sounds different).

Seemingly self-evident concepts require differentiation as well, including basic colors such as blue. A historical analysis of over 78 languages found that most cultures identify colors over time, with blue consistently named last.[2] This means that most cultures, despite sensing blue for thousands of years, were not describing anything as blue. Why? The hypothesis is that notwithstanding the blue sky and ocean, there aren't enough naturally blue things to warrant differentiating them. The Egyptians are the exception and, as it turns out, were one of earliest cultures to invent blue dye.[3] For everyone else, it took a long time for the concept of blue to matter enough to name it. This happened with the color orange too in the English language. While Europe has had orange sunsets and orange fall foliage for thousands of years, Europeans simply referred to those colors (including pumpkins and anything else orange) as red-yellow. It wasn't until the arrival of orange the fruit that they started calling orange things "orange"; as a result, it was orange the fruit that came before orange the color. People simply didn't feel that the color was worth differentiating until oranges came along.[4]

Differentiating things, however, is not the same as having taste. If it were, we could just perform chemical analyses on wine and compare the levels of acids. Taste also requires a subjective lens, as demonstrated by our sommelier's observation that the wine "overpowers the hors d'oeuvres." With this statement, he doesn't just describe the wine but also communicates a lived experience. And although rudimentary, our social drinker demonstrates taste as well by "liking" the wine. This sentiment simultaneously differentiates the wine from other beverages (which are presumably disliked) through a subjective lens ("liking" things in general).

A subjective lens can incorporate almost every dimension of the human experience. Did your fiancé propose with a ring in your glass, making it the "best" wine ever? Totally valid. Did the vineyard owner donate to your least favorite politician, "causing" the wine to be unpalatable? This counts too. As the philosopher David Hume described it, the subjective component is like 1,000 men with different sentiments who are all right, because "beauty is not a quality in things themselves; it exists merely in the mind that contemplates them, and each mind perceives a different beauty."[5] In other words, there is no wrong way to have taste.

And so we arrive at the twin pillars of taste: differentiation and subjectivity. And while it's provocative to imagine that we could somehow extract raw taste data from our heads, it's just as well that we can't (none of us need to know that Uncle Bob hates Cole Porter because his dentist played Porter's music). Instead, we're left organizing taste ourselves using two predictable techniques: editorial and curation.

Organizing Taste

In practice, there are two main ways we organize our taste. The first is editorial. If you've ever liked something on Facebook, tweeted on Twitter, or rated a product on Amazon, then you've organized like an editor. Editorial has an "in" and "out" group. If you "like" something on Facebook, then that content is in. If you don't, then it's out. If an editor at the *New York Times* thinks that an article is fit to print, then it's in. If not, then it is out. Same for literary editors; if they think a book is good, then they acquire it, and it's in. If not, then it's out.

Curation is the second way to organize subjectively. For example, if you've ever made pinboards on Pinterest, playlists on Spotify, or galleries on Facebook, then you've organized like a curator. Curation has two or more groups of content arranged subjectively (Figure 3.3). As a result, while a song may be unfit for one playlist, a curator has the power to find or create a different playlist.

You might be surprised how often you curate already; when you get dressed in the morning, your outfit is a collection of clothes you curated. The decor in the various rooms of your home is a collection of furniture and objects you curated. The dishes you prepared for dinner make up a meal you curated. We curate all the time.

Academia embraces curation as well (although academia doesn't quite call it that). Many fields—including psychology, cognitive science, and cognitive anthropology—utilize a research method called "pile sorting" that, in research methods jargon, means curating content into collections. For example, a researcher administering a pile-sorting task may ask participants to arrange a pile of words printed on index cards into groups that make the most sense to them. Take a list of foods such as chicken, fish, salad, pasta, brownies, and milk. One person may lump brownies and milk together because they're complementary. Another may lump pasta and brownies

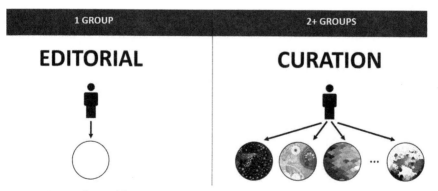

Figure 3.3   Editorial has one "in" group. Curation has many "in" groups.

together because they're comfort foods. The same person could also put fish and salad together, because in that person's mind they taste best fresh. What's important is that the pile maker makes a subjective evaluation about what he or she thinks goes well together (essentially, to curate).

But so what? Who cares that editorial lumps things into an in group and that curation clumps them into two or more groups? What does that have to do with the problem of discovery?

Curation Scales Subjectivity

If editorial is like drawing with pencil, then curation—and the ability to subjectively organize content into two or more groups—is like painting in color. To start, it means that there is no upper limit to the quantity and creativity of organization (Figure 3.4). Curation allows for as many subjective patterns, relationships, and similarities as we want. It allows us to make as many outfits, meals, playlists, and galleries as we can imagine.

Editorial has no such freedom. If I'm an editor at the *New York Times,* it's my job to publish "all the news that's fit to print." If I'm an engineer at BMW, it's my job to develop the "ultimate driving machine." If I'm tweeting for the Food Network, I need to tweet about pasta sauces. These editorial and branding mandates require adherence to a singular goal. And that's the primary strength of an editorial voice: a clear, focused, and singular message.

This is also the primary weakness an editorial voice.

Curation creates rich tapestries of tastes capable of containing all the perspectives in the world. It's limited only by the boundaries of our imagination, perception, and curiosity. For example, on Pinterest, the top influencers have 62 boards on average, while the average user with 25,000 followers has

EDITORIAL   **CURATION**

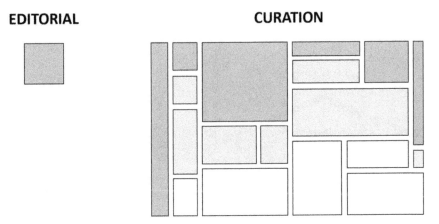

Figure 3.4

around 108 boards.[6] And it's this flexibility to scale beyond editorial's in and out groups that enables curation to be more expressive and detailed; it's like subjectivity but in high definition (HD).

Curation Is Subjectivity in HD

Curation is the MRI scan of subjectivity: it reveals the never before seen structure of our tastes and makes editorial data look crude and one-dimensional in comparison. Take the editorial action of liking something on Facebook: after liking Iggy Azalea, Burberry, and a few hundred other things, you end up with a giant warehouse of likes. Your credit card history is another example. After buying a few hundred items, you end up with a muddled warehouse of purchases.

And while these disorderly warehouses do provide some insight into your tastes, it turns out to be a very low-resolution view. As far as the credit card company knows, you bought those Barbie Dolls for yourself, not for your son to bring as a gift to his cousin's birthday party. And as far as Facebook knows, you really like Wendy's hamburgers, not that you have a sweet tooth and Wendy's ran a promotion where if you like Wendy's on Facebook you get a free ice cream. When everything you buy or like is tossed into the large, undifferentiated editorial in pile, the context behind why you bought it and why you liked it is lost. All we know is that for what could be any reason, you bought or liked something.

Curation is the opposite. Curation preserves the meaning and purpose behind our selections. Far from creating ever larger warehouses, curation builds a house filled with many rooms of preferences (Figure 3.5). In these rooms, we see people arrange, appreciate, and contextualize the content in their lives. We see a room for "dolls I've purchased for my children," a room for "model trains I've purchased for myself," and a room for "things I liked because I got something free." It's insight in HD and a clear representation of our tastes, values, and understanding. And it's what Google, Facebook, Twitter, and recommendation algorithms completely fail to capture.

Low Resolution

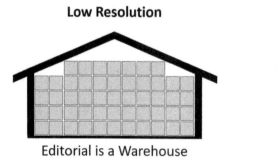

Editorial is a Warehouse

High Resolution

Curation is a Home

Figure 3.5

Curation Marries Scope and Focus

The Dewey decimal system, the global phone system, and Google successfully married scope and focus to find books, call people, and search for web pages, respectively. How could the union of a different scope and focus help us discover things we love? What would it look like to index everything in the world, not in terms of codes, phone numbers, or keywords but in terms of human subjectivity?

I'll tell you: it looks like curation. Curation is the part of ourselves that we've yet to bring online in the same way we've brought our friendships to Facebook or professional ties to LinkedIn. It's our fascinations, curiosities, dreams, and desires that we crave to discover in others. It's our subjective identity.

And it's humanizing the web: no longer will marketers need to blindly approximate our interests by targeting our gender, income bracket, or zip code. No longer will we have to suffer Uncle Bob's political rants on Twitter in order to catch pictures of his new horses and maple syrup distillery. For the first time, curation sets the stage to solve the problem of discovery by harnessing the richest source of subjective data that most closely mirrors the web of subjective connections in our own minds: the curated collection (Figure 3.6). And we've only just started to unlock its potential.

As an example of further unlocking curation's potential, Pinterest enabled the ability to create sections within pinboards, announced in 2017.[7] Far beyond the basic warehousing and editorial of liking things, having sections

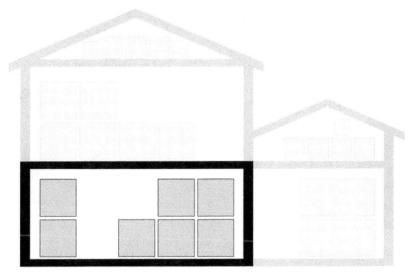

Figure 3.6

within collections is like offering architects the ability to make towns out of houses. For example, you can use sections to break the pinboard dream house into sections for kitchen, living room, master bedroom, foyer, backyard, furnished basement, and nursery. Or you could create a pinboard on fall fashion, with sections dedicated to jackets, scarves, hats, and gloves. Ideas from Pinterest's announcement include "Secret shopping: Start a secret board with sections for each person who's getting a gift this season. Friendly feasting: Organize your Friendsgiving board by main courses, sides, pies and wines. Lots of layers: Move your winter styles to a new board with sections for warm sweaters, tall boots, wool coats and more. Deck the halls: Light up your home with decoration ideas organized by each room in the house."[8] When it comes to marrying scope and focus and unlocking the power of subjectivity online, innovation is already happening.

Curation Unlocks Subjectivity

> When we curate, we are enhancing a connection in the global neural network we are inadvertently creating.
>
> Eliot Van Buskirk, data storyteller at Spotify

When we curate, we create the opportunity for others to discover from us. When others curate, they create the opportunity for us to discover from them. And when we curate together, we create the opportunity to delight in and collaborate with our shared passions (Figure 3.7). Like a trade secret to a mysterious process we only recently learned existed, curation lifts the shroud of mystery surrounding one of the greatest parts of human subjectivity. And it sets the stage for a renaissance in subjective discovery not seen since Google learned to harness the hyperlink.

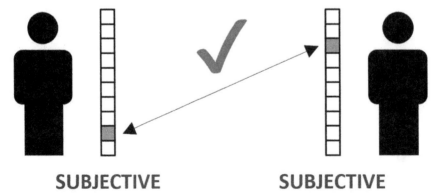

SUBJECTIVE   **SUBJECTIVE**

Figure 3.7   Curation enables subjective, taste-based matching.

Soon, "friending" and "following" people will make about as much sense for content discovery as using Lycos or Dogpile does for web search. Connecting to all of someone and to everything that crosses the person's mind will seem like a painfully blunt approach compared to the precision offered by a curated approach. This curated future lays the groundwork for a post-social web whereby who someone is isn't as important as the quality of her or his interests. If you haven't already seen this trend coming, don't worry: you will. As William Gibson, who coined the term "cyberspace," wrote, "the future is already here—it's just not evenly distributed."[9]

Curation Is a Powder Keg

Since 2011, curation rocketed in popularity, with Pinterest measuring as the fastest-growing website of all time—and no one knows what will happen next.[10] The curation awakening that Pinterest popularized spread like wildfire across the web, with Erin Griffith (now at the *New York Times*) writing that "If imitation is the sincerest form of flattery the founders of Pinterest must be blushing their asses off. . . . Pinterest Pinterest Pinterest. It's spread like a hot, juicy rumor . . . , infecting (or improving, depending on how you look at it) the way we use the Internet."[11]

And it's only curation's opening act. It's worth remembering that while Google was easily the 15th search engine company to launch, it crushed its competitors by leveraging the subjectivity found in links. With the rich veins of subjective "gold" stored in today's ever-growing mountains of curation data, it's only a matter of time before the next "Google" learns to harness it: the powder keg of curation has yet to blow. But if we've learned anything about the trail of technological innovation in subjectivity, the status quo won't last for long.

The only question is, when content overload becomes a thing of the past, will you be among the winners or the losers of a humanized web? Get ready: in the next section you'll learn how curation changes how you'll make, buy, and sell everything.

PART 2

Curation Changes How You Make, Buy, and Sell Everything

Introduction to Part II
Curation Means Business

As more and more information is thrown at us, we are now ironically often seeking less and less of it. And this is perhaps what the next great wave of tech and info billionaires will address—as curators whose purpose will be to find greater meaning, context, and relevancy in this mass information world.

Anthony K. Tjan, *New York Times* best-selling author and founder of the venture capital firm Cue Ball

The movements of fads, fashions, tastes, and preferences are mysterious. Sometimes the preferences of groups large and small seem rational and predictable—and at other times capricious and arbitrary. This makes the $2.2 trillion creative industry volatile and full of opportunity (Figure II.1).[1]

Sales, web page views, and increasingly the number of streams are the gold standard of measuring the tastes and interests of the masses. Top 10 lists and trending data dominate the discussion of what the market wants. However, these indicators capture aggregate tastes and are lagging indicators; there's no guarantee that the tastes of today will be the tastes of tomorrow. But we're used to that. It's been the status quo for a long time.

The social web measures aggregate tastes with unprecedented speed and accuracy. We can tally the likes, tweets, and favorites of millions, revealing popular movements in real time. Still however, like sales, page views, and streams, the social web remains an aggregate measure of a lagging indicator; there's no guarantee that the likes of today will be the likes of tomorrow. And we're familiar with that too: it's been the status quo for a while.

Curation is changing this. Not only do curated collections map the cultural landscape in high definition, but they also reveal the curators leading

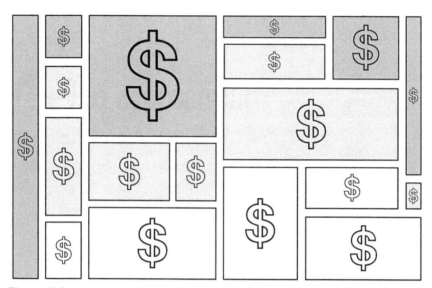

Figure II.1

the charge. Beyond tracking the birth and growth of niche and medium-size markets, curation allows us to identify the curators who found and develop these audiences. And these curators do more than synchronize communities; they are the bellwethers and catalysts of the "next thing," shaking the foundations of traditional marketing to the core.

Curation-Based Business Models

The network structure of the Internet is a massive disintermediator; like telephones, any connection can connect to any other connection at any time. Unfortunately, instead of one call happening at a time, the Internet is more like a trillion simultaneous calls. In the wake of this cacophony came new technologies and business models that reintermediated us with content and each other. For example, search engines are an intermediary for networked information. You almost never go to information directly (who types in URLs?); instead, you "Google it."

Curation is another form or reintermediation and creates business models too. One example is the Pinterest influencer talent agency company HelloSociety, which was acquired by the *New York Times*'s native advertising division in 2016.[2] HelloSociety noticed that pinners were cutting deals with marketers and started a technology-enabled talent agency to represent pinners and provide better campaign performance tooling to brands (think charts that show brands how many clicks a curator delivered). To give a sense of the magnitude of dollars involved, in 2014 the top pinners on Pinterest made about $250,000 a year. HelloSociety was able to enter into the space and generate $12.5 million in revenue with 26 employees the same year.

HelloSociety was a well-executed idea with great timing. Kyla Brenna founded HelloSociety in 2012 while working as an executive assistant within the Los Angeles–based start-up incubator Science.[3] In between her duties as an executive assistant, she observed that one of the e-commerce shops, Uncovet, attracted large numbers of buyers from Pinterest, many more than from Facebook or search. "It was this really highly converting traffic that was resulting in the majority of their sales; organic traffic coming from the fact that people liked their products and were pinning them."[4] So, Brennan started to perform some tests and reached out directly to the disproportionately influential pinners on Pinterest. She found that the impact of these pinners was huge: "One pin would send thousands—sometimes tens of thousands—of unique visits, and it would result in sales that were so much higher than they were from Facebook and Twitter, and sometimes even from search. It was crazy."[5]

To measure this impact, Brennan reached out to pinners and asked them to continue pinning whatever they wanted but provided a special tracking code that would track if purchases happened through their pins; she found that the pins were resulting in real sales across a variety of stores. She then leveraged that data and reached out to companies to see if they wanted to launch a marketing campaign with the impactful pinners: "So I just started cold-calling companies that I thought would be a good fit and asking if they wanted to work with some of the top Pinterest users. And that's how it started."[6] Today, HelloSociety manages over 1,500 tastemakers and influencers across multiple social media platforms, running campaigns for top brands. One campaign that HelloSociety ran is for Reebok, promoting its newly launched athleisure apparel line. HelloSociety coordinated with Pinterest influencers who were well positioned to show how Reebok fits into their busy lives. Compared to Reebok's average campaign on Instagram, the company saw 101 percent more repins with the Pinterest influencers.[7]

Other businesses, rather than making money from curators, bake curation into the product experience itself. For example, there are now mobile-first e-commerce companies with curation at their core that are experiencing astronomical growth. For example, while Amazon and Alibaba are absolute titans in e-commerce, e-commerce in total represents just 8 percent and 16 percent, respectively, of the total $9 trillion retail market in the United States and China; while Amazon's and Alibaba's warehouse approach scales impressively offer "everything" at low prices, the search experience they offer for finding things to buy remains insufficient to capture the entire market.[8] Hans Tung, a venture capitalist at GGV Capital, has an investment thesis that uses curation to drive a competitive advantage in an e-commerce landscape dominated by undifferentiated e-commerce warehouses. GGV Capital is based in both the United States and China with $3.8 billion under management and has several curation-first e-commerce companies in its portfolio. In Tung's words,

> Differentiating from the guerillas begins with search vs. discovery. Amazon and Taobao are giant virtual warehouses that rely upon purpose-based shopping. Consumers visit these sites to find a product they know they want, and can buy for a low price. Consumers log on, search for an item, buy it and leave. . . . E-brands and vertical marketplaces aren't going to compete with this kind of warehouse search. Instead, they focus on discovery—curating a body of products in a specific category that customers want to peruse and occasionally purchase. Mobile shopping is becoming entertainment, and a well curated group of products makes for a more enjoyable experience. Online brands are approaching curation in different ways and their popularity is evident in the app store.[9]

All three curated e-commerce companies in Tung's portfolio are in the top 10 most downloaded apps in the retail category of the app store. On April 1, 2017, Wish was number 2, OfferUp number 3, and Poshmark number 8. "None of these apps target the shoppers who feel they need access to every single product right now. But they do offer consumers a curated experience—by product or price—to discover affordable luxury products in apps built for the endless entertainment of smartphone users."[10]

Curators are able to create outsize impact because they fundamentally understand what their audience wants better than any outsiders. And we're just at the beginning of seeing how curatorial knowledge transforms marketing from the inside out.

CHAPTER FOUR

Curators Transform Marketing

Curators Know Their Market

> I have never read a comprehensive definition of the word *collection,* but one might set out a working definition as "an obsession organized."
> Aristes, "Calm and Uncollected," *American Scholar,* 1988

Lauren Zwanziger is a style journalist and started using Pinterest to organize her fashion and interior design discoveries while a fashion design student in Tennessee. She browsed fashion blogs and other pinboards on Pinterest and curated her favorites into inspiration boards, a process of design thinking required by many of her classes—she even curated her senior collection project on Pinterest. Then something unexpected happened; she went from 200 to 27,000 followers overnight. Zwanziger wasn't writing blog posts or tweeting snarky remarks about celebrities; she was sharing her unique taste with the world—and the world wanted more.[1]

Publishers hire editors, editors work with literary agents, record companies employ professionals in A&R (artists and repertoire), and marketers engage with cool hunters: these roles exist to map the cultural landscape for firms in creative industries. They're also losing relevance because of curators such as Zwanziger.

Like Wikipedia did to encyclopedias, curation by the crowds puts pressure on any marketing, advertising, consulting, or professional group that claims to know what's in or what's next. For many reasons, the wisdom of the curating crowds has much better knowledge of diverse, fluctuating tastes than small groups of professionals (Figure 4.1).

Many successful curators curate for an audience of one (themselves), and it can come as a surprise that other people share their tastes (it's their secret to outpacing the professionals). Take Shayla Moller from Provo, Utah, as an

☐ CURATORS   ■ PROFESSIONALS

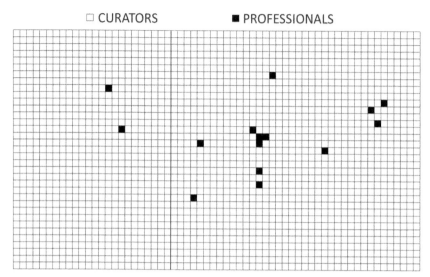

Figure 4.1   Professionals can't represent the diversity of interests that legions of curators can.

example. Professionally she's a designer at Skullcandy, but as a curator she has 2.6 million followers on Pinterest through her collections with names such as "People," "Home," and "Music and Its Makers." From her point of view, "it's still strange to me to think I have that many followers or that many people who could like what I like. . . . As in, I like to only pin aesthetically pleasing images and to keep it looking really pretty. Or at least what I think is pretty."[2] For Moller, it doesn't require an agenda per se; her natural tastes set the agenda across 34 pinboards. She says that "I've never really thought about what defines my Pinterest style. . . . I just pin anything that I'm drawn to! I do think I'm interested and intrigued by a lot of different styles, but then I always love seeing how they still seem to flow when I see all of my pins together."

For Amy Sia, a freelance artist from Melbourne, Australia, and a Pinterest curator with 200,000 followers, the sentiment is equally personal. She's not there to sell anything; she just wants to share what's interesting to her. She explains that "I guess it is just my point of view. I try to pin only things I love and am genuinely interested in!"[3]

Astric Campos doesn't try to optimize the time of day she posts her pins (as many social media marketers try to do) but instead curates what and when she feels it the most. She trusts her instincts, saying that "I just pin images that inspire me for that time of day. I'd like to think that is also what appeals to my readers because it's a bit of an inspirational theme. I enjoy pinning this way, I trust my intuition and it comes out more organic, as if I am telling a short story."[4] This approach has garnered her over 900,000 followers.

Helena Casanovas shares this sentiment too. For her over 420,000 followers on Pinterest across boards such as "Kids Fashion," "Kids Bedding," and "My Little Boy Loves it," she leans heavily on her own aesthetic: "My boards are a reflection of what I like and I enjoy creating them. Creativity can be found everywhere!"[5] To be successful as a curator and outpace the professionals, leaning on your personal taste can be a competitive advantage.

Even Curation Playing Field

As more and more content lives on the Internet, today's amateur curator is just as likely to discover the "next thing" as a professional. New artists break on YouTube, and future best-selling authors bootstrap their careers off blogs. Products, games, and media launch on Kickstarter with funding by the fans who discover and believe in them. For Zwanziger, she had access to many of the same fashion runway results and interior design photography as most magazine professionals, equipping her with the raw materials to craft her unique point of view. Curators evaluate the same up-and-coming work as the professionals, and this has leveled the playing field of discovery.

Before the Internet, it was much more possible to be exhaustive in the search for new things. For example, pre-Internet music fans could scour every record shop in their city; while time-consuming, it was actually possible to canvas all of them and get a pulse on the music scene. For the interior design field until around 2007 in New York City, as designer Katherine Bragg describes it, it was still possible to conduct a practically exhaustive search for items for new projects. She'd visit all the relevant design fairs, shops, flea markets, and showrooms and review all the magazines coming out at that time, which combined gave her a "total" view of the market. Not only would it give her the most informed perspective to do her job the best and the satisfaction of being "complete," but it also created the confidence that if a client came in with some ideas/pieces of her or his own, she would be in the position of having already seen, evaluated, and rejected it for the project; it was easier to establish curatorial authority.

For Bragg today, much of the searching for new projects takes place on curation platforms such as Pinterest and e-commerce platforms such as 1stdibs. And while it's technically possible to search every product page on a limited, speciality e-commerce shop such as 1stdibs, there's no way to search everything on Pinterest. As a result, the set of options is impossibly large for one person, making it more difficult to establish an entirely complete view. You can spend 10 times as much time now searching out content in an endless digital ocean, and your client can still approach you with something he or she found within five minutes on Pinterest that you haven't seen before.

Public Record

The Internet threw open the closed doors of curation, and today's amateur curators have never been more public. Before moving online, curation was largely a home-bound activity. But with more and more websites encouraging people to clip, collect, and pin their discoveries, we benefit from each other's curatorial expertise more than ever before. And in Zwanziger's case, a lot more: she has over 4 million followers today.

Diversity of Tastes

The population and diversity of curators exploded with the introduction of Internet curation tools. With over 150 million users on Pinterest alone, these global armies of curators vastly overwhelm the proprietary work of professionals in both volume and detail. Faced with the daunting task of making sense of "everything," it's increasingly looking possible only by the awe-inspiring abilities of "everyone."

Curators Know What's Next

What style of pants or cars will people want in six months? Predicting demand is notoriously difficult when tastes seem to move with the wind (Figure 4.2). And the risks are very real; arriving at the correct answer can mean the difference between a hit product and a dud.

The primary reason marketers, A&R reps, art curators, dealers, buyers, and agents study the cultural landscape is to track trends and make calculated bets about what's next. With honed intuitions and market research in hand, these professionals try to get inside our heads.

But with millions of curators on the web, marketers don't need to try to get inside our heads anymore: we're letting them in. Curated collections present

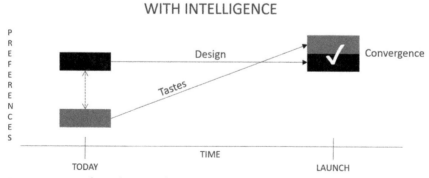

Figure 4.2   Today's designs aligned with tomorrow's taste.

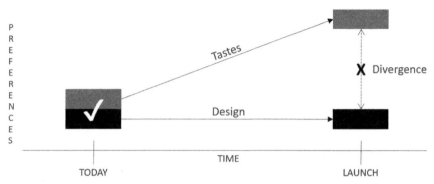

Figure 4.3   Today's designs misaligned with tomorrow's taste.

our tastes to the world, ranging from "My Dream Kitchen" to "Books I Need." While today's professionals at best approximate market preferences, curators authentically reveal them (Figure 4.3); they're the "voice of the market"— ideal surrogate consumers whose preferences aren't only the most demanding but also the most representative. One wonders if a marketer need only ask a curator "what do you want?" to peer into the future desires of a broader audience.

Measuring Trends with Pinterest

Pinterest is no stranger to the value of its own data; the company knows that its sitting on top of the collective knowledge of hundreds of millions of shopping, planning, and discovering curators. As part of the Pinterest for Business division, the company analyzed this data to produce trend reports for the upcoming year. "Pinterest has a unique advantage when it comes to trends. We see trends bubble up based on what 200 million Pinners are searching and saving around the world. They aren't just passing fads to 'like' or look at. They're ideas people are trying in real life and planning to do in the future."[6] To make predictions for 2018, Pinterest for Business analyzed over 100 billion ideas to find the ones that met three quantitative criteria of trending at the end of 2017. The first criteria is that the topic gained a critical mass. By "critical mass," they mean that the idea reached a certain absolute size. For example, while some topics may have grown exponentially, witnessing an increase of 10,000 percent in popularity, if that growth was from 1 to 100 people, it still wouldn't meet the absolute size minimum. For this study, Pinterest set the absolute threshold to 250,000 saves for a topic, globally. The second criteria is that the trend must have grown at a rate of 50 percent or greater, year after year. So, for example, a trend that grew from

166,666 likes to 250,000 over 2017 would be eligible, but one that grew from 250,000 to 300,000 (which, despite being a lot of growth, is lower than the 50 percent threshold) would not. The final criteria is a "strong upward trend during the final 3–6 months of the year (not including seasonal spikes)." So it's not enough to just grow 50 percent from 166,000 to 250,000 over the year; the growth must also be accelerating into the end of the year, producing proportionally more likes at the end than at the beginning. The final outcome is a list of ideas trending at the start of 2018 that Pinterest pitches as "an idea sparker, to-try list, 'work' book, personal assistant, and 2018 muse," with uses across "your content, marketing, merchandising, and even product development."

Companies are already leveraging these trends to drive value. For example, the arts and crafts retailer Michaels Stores (which has over 1,500 locations) uses curator trends to develop products before competitors. In 2017, Michaels created a do-it-yourself "Make It Kit" for shibori cloth (essentially, Japanese tie dye), capturing that trend at the register as it took off online. On the content side, when Hewlitt-Packard learned that printable artwork was a strong trend on Pinterest, Hewlitt-Packard harnessed it by producing pins with free printable art. On the retail side, CB2 (the hip, modern division of Crate and Barrel) leveraged a prediction from a 2017 report that "navy is the new black" and created in-store signage educating people of the style trend as part of its new navy-colored product line.[7] For 2018 in food, here are some of the trends that Pinterest identified. Do they resonate with you? The list includes snap peas (+273 percent growth); Moroccan food (+2,579 percent); souping, which is essentially making soup (+306 percent); Korean condiments (+222 percent); plant proteins (+417 percent); and air fryers, which is a healthier way to fry food using convection heating (+1,809 percent). I looked back at the 2017 trend report to see if it made sense to me today. That report called out jackfruit as a meat substitute (Mellisa's Produce reports a 30 percent increase in sales over the year from May 2017),[8] *sous-vide*–style cooking (I've definitely had friends picking up *sous-vides,* so that passes my gut check), and healthy chips such as sweet potato chips or zucchini chips (those have always been popular in my book). The predictions from 2017 seem to pass a general level of scrutiny, making the 2018 predictions all the more interesting.

Curators Protect Their Audiences

Nearly half of all Americans consume news from Facebook.[9] So when Facebook fired its news curators—and its algorithms started promoting fake articles two months before Donald Trump won the presidency—it's not surprising that the *New York Times* reported that "Silicon Valley landed on the

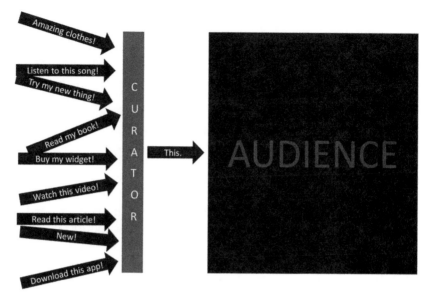

Figure 4.4 Curators are the new gate-keepers.

idea that widespread misinformation spread online was a primary factor in the race's outcome."[10] It's estimated that the top 20 fake news articles were more popularly consumed than the top 20 legitimate articles.[11] The *New York Times* called it "Facebook's damage to democracy."[12] Barack Obama didn't mince words either, saying that "in an age where there's so much active misinformation and it looks the same when you see it on a Facebook page . . . , then we don't know what to protect."[13]

Curators protect their audience's from bad content (Figure 4.4). One former Facebook news curator described the raw algorithmic results as "a garbage fire."[14] For news in particular, preventing lies and hoaxes is paramount. Ensuring accuracy, however, is not why the Facebook news curation team was fired (they filtered hoaxes quite well). They were fired because of their liberal slant.[15] The irony is that every professional news organizations has a slant: it's called a perspective, and it's part of the definition of "editorial." In the world of subjectivity, the way you protect audiences from one perspective is to provide them with a full chorus of perspectives. Instead of removing human judgment, Facebook needed, as CNN reported, better curation.[16] For example, Facebook needed to fully curate the range of perspectives that we know exist from top editorial sources such as *The Economist,* the *New York Times,* and *Mother Jones* (not the back-room censorship in which they did participate). Removing human judgment out of a naive conception of "impartiality" merely handed the asylum to the inmates.

The Curator Gatekeeper

Many industries are defined by curators' ability to protect their audience. Take fashion, for example: an executive at *Vogue* magazine develops a reputation for accepting only the best. She says "no" most of the time, and her readers love her discriminating taste. When she's in charge, people know they get a magazine of exceptional quality. And if a dress by a new designer gets published, that designer celebrates knowing that she made it to the big leagues.

When working well, curators are a lot like magazine executives. They are the frontline filters who say "yes" selectively and "no" frequently. And when they earn the trust of audiences, they earn their attention.

For anyone with something to sell, content to share, or ideas to spread, curators are the new gatekeepers. And like gatekeepers in traditional industries (editors, buyers, reporters, radio hosts, etc.), there is considerable value in their approval—and considerable difficulty in getting it.

Like proposing a segment to National Public Radio or pitching a product to Walmart, working with curator-gatekeepers presents unique challenges and rewards. One challenge is that there are few formal channels with which to engage them. One emerging channel is the influencer marketing firm HelloSociety, which connects brands to talented Pinterest users and their unique audiences.[17] When done well, it's possible for a brand to pinpoint its target audiences where the curators want their content as much as they want their audiences.

Gatekeepers Protect Audiences and Earn Their Trust

Jillian Tohber Leslie is a curator on Pinterest with over 770,000 followers. She founded Catch My Party, a curated resource for themed parties that turned from a side project into a full-time job for both her and her husband. Previously, Leslie was a writer in Hollywood and her husband an employee at MySpace. As professionals who worked in media, they bring a lot of strategy to their curation process. When Leslie gives advice to prospective curators, she puts it in terms of focusing on the brand: "I think it's really important to understand what your brand is, and to really stick to it . . . if you're a food blogger that does desserts, I want to see photos of your desserts. I don't want to see photos of your kids at the pool. Even though you have lovely children and a cool looking pool, I follow you because you make delicious desserts."[18] It's critical to understand your audience and their expectations from you. As Leslie puts it, "it's really understanding the kind of value you're putting out into the world, and going deep into that."

In an information environment where content of varying relevance comes at people from all directions, nothing is more appreciated than the protection a curator offers. When audiences feel protected by a curator, they end up trusting their selections, which confer to curators another ability: the power to propel creators to success by endorsing their content.

Curators Endorse You

It's one thing to write a book—it's another to be in Oprah's Book Club. When curators select your content, their gravitas accrues to your content. As gatekeepers, they can propel previously unknown content into the consciousness of many.

For example, the playlist curator Sean Parker (the Napster cofounder) was instrumental in launching the musical artist Lorde. Before Lorde sold millions of albums and was played on every major radio station to hundreds of millions, she was just another unknown musician with an album on Spotify—that is, until Parker curated her single "Royals" to his playlist "Hipster International."[19] Within six days, "Royals" broke through to the Spotify Viral Chart. With the song's noticeable viral growth, Spotify began explicitly promoting Lorde across the network, and her popularity soared into superstardom; not bad for being curated into the right playlist. And this trend is only set to continue, as Spotify users currently spend about 50 percent of their listening time tuning into playlists that they or others make. This creates a phenomenon for artists whereby according to music business development manager James Walsh, who works at the digital music distributor Ditto Music, "every artist wants a spot on the high-traffic playlists like Today's Top Hits or Rap Caviar. There's an official pitch process, a form anyone can fill out with details about their track and their hopes and dreams for world-beating success."[20] Placement on a Spotify playlist such as "Today's Top Hits" or "RapCaviar" can change an an artist's career. In a study by the European Commission, placement on one of these playlists can yield up to 20 million streams at a value per track of up to $163,000.[21]

Curators gain this power by holding not just the attention of their audience but also their trust. While anyone with a budget can buy ad impressions and shove their message in front of people, there's almost no way an advertisement can forge trust, especially since the channel itself can even imply manipulation (why is BP Oil advertising how environmentally sound it is?). Curation brings with it the endorsement of curators and the trust they confer.

AWAL (the acronym for "artists without a label") is a digital-first music label that specializes in placing songs on prominent playlists on streaming music sites. While there are more than 2 billion playlists on Spotify, AWAL "can help lift a song, and the artist behind it, from obscurity" with placement in the right playlist.[22] For example, the artist Guordan Banks received around 20,000 streams every two weeks until selected by the "Chilled R&B" playlist, at which point streams more than doubled to about 50,000. After being featured on the "Are & Be" playlist, that count nearly quadrupled to 200,000, almost peaking at 300,000. After being reinserted to "Are & Be" several more times, the track ended up peaking at 500,000 streams every two weeks. For typical artists in its roster, AWAL says that they "generally see a boost of 50 percent to 100 percent once they get on Spotify-sponsored playlists." And those boosts, while spikey at first, translate into consistent streams afterward, with artists seeing a "20 percent increase in their streams" after their playlist rotation.

The power of a curator's trust can demonstrably impact the bottom line. But this power impacts the bottom line in more ways as well. Specifically, a curator can enlarge the stature of the product itself.

Curators Enlarge You

Albert Einstein's *Foundations of the General Theory of Relativity,* Sir Isaac Newton's *Principia,* your physics dissertation; Jay-Z's "Empire State of Mind," Kanye West's "Gold Digger," your hip hop single; Apple's iPhone, Samsung's Galaxy, your new smartphone: association is a powerful force (Figure 4.5).

And curators wield it. Curation harnesses the power of association to enlarge content. For example, the right association may confer legitimacy with comparison to established works. It can also attract unanticipated audiences. Like a musician who's originally unpopular in her or his home country and becomes huge in Japan, curated associations can resonate with new markets in significant and surprising ways. For all manner of crossover hits or establishing new hits, curation and the power of association is an important ingredient in enlarging content's appeal.

Michael Moskowitz, founder of the online marketplace Bureau of Trade, proved this in dollars and cents. His approach was to take auction items on eBay and curate them with high-end imagery and article-quality descriptions. For example, imagine a collage featuring an Italian coastline, a Ducati

Figure 4.5

motorcycle, and beautiful people wearing vintage leather jackets—with those jackets then linking to an eBay auction. And the results were undeniable: items curated by the Bureau of Trade sold from 50 percent to 100 percent more on eBay than the same items that lacked curation.[23] With curation's value clear, eBay acquired the company and transformed the eBay home page into an entirely curated experience.

Hollywood is no stranger to using the associative power of curation to enlarge its own products as well. Each year, a relatively small group of Hollywood industry professionals vote for the movies to win Oscar awards across a variety of categories including "Best Picture." Interestingly, though, the opinions of the industry professionals rarely overlap with the popular opinions of audiences; only four movies that topped the popular charts over the past 30 years (13 percent of the top-grossing films) also won for best picture: they were *Rain Man* (1988), *Forrest Gump* (1994), *Titanic* (1997) and *The Lord of Rings: The Return of the King* (2003).[24] That number fell to zero in the past 14 years, with no films from the top 10 most popular winning for best picture; the opinions of professionals have not just been largely different from the opinions of most of us but diverge further still.

According to film historian Jonathan Kuntz from the University of California– Los Angeles, there are several possible reasons for this. One is that instead of voting based on popularity, industry professionals are more interested in acknowledging contributions to the cinematic arts, such as technical or artistic innovation or cultural impact. Another possibility is that the awards function as a means for the film industry to bring attention (and dollars) to films that aren't already popular. As Kuntz points out, "The Academy Award has always been, since the early days, Hollywood's way of helping itself in promoting films. . . . The value of an Oscar to a medium or small film can be great, whereas to a large film, it can be insignificant."[25] For example, in 2009 the movie *Avatar* became the highest-grossing film of all time, launching 3D films into the mainstream. Yet *The Hurt Locker,* a film set during the Iraq War, won for best picture. This brings up the question, how good must *The Hurt Locker* be to be better than that box office record-breaking, technically and experientially impressive *Avatar* to win for best picture? In another example, *Star Wars: The Force Awakens,* released in 2015, broke box office records, grossing $970 million domestically. Yet *Spotlight,* a story about investigative journalists, won for best picture but grossed only $47 million. Again, how good must *Spotlight* be to be better than *Star Wars?* The answer is of course that it may not be; rather, curators (the Academy of Motion Picture Arts and Sciences in this case) have the power to enlarge content by making comparisons.

Whereas Hollywood may reveal its tastes and agenda when it votes for the Oscars, individual curators reveal their tastes and interests as well. And this creates an unprecedented opportunity to find audiences who share the same preferences through taste targeting.

Taste Targeting

"Half the money I spend on advertising is wasted; the trouble is I don't know which half," goes the famous John Wanamaker quote that explains that the advertising industry wastes money hand over fist (that this point goes unadvertised should come as no surprise). When it comes to allocating the $500 billion spent by the ad industry in 2013, figuring out which half is wasted is big business.[26] Google, Facebook, Twitter, and practically half of Silicon Valley are almost entirely funded by advertisers trying to spend ad dollars more effectively.

To that end, Facebook offers the ability to target people based on their schools, towns, or likes. Google's primary solution targets people based on their web searches. What does curation offer?

Curation offers the ability to target people by their tastes (Figure 4.6). Reflect for a moment on what Google was able to accomplish with the little bit of subjective data stored in links. Now imagine the possibilities with the rich veins of subjective data stored in curated collections and the implications of effective taste targeting.

Say that you're trying to sell a high-performance blender that you think owners of KitchenAid mixers will like. Traditional ad targeting might select females with discretionary income who read cooking magazines and live in the suburbs. Editorial data, such as the likes data on Facebook, could allow additional precision by targeting people who've already liked KitchenAid mixers.

Curation data takes it further. Not only can you target people who like KitchenAid mixers, but you can also distinguish the ones who bought it in baby blue for their retro kitchens versus the ones who bought it in chrome

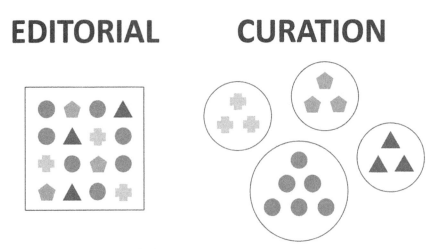

Figure 4.6   Curation unlocks taste targeting.

for their sleek and modern kitchens. You can identify others who cook infrequently, because they seemingly got their mixer as part of a wedding registry, and others still who bake a lot, with hundreds of recipes for cakes and cookies.

Taste targeting enables advertisers to truly identify the people with the greatest likelihood of actually liking their offering. As it turns out, the high-performance blender you're trying to sell has a chrome finish that likely appeals to the modern kitchen and bakes-frequently taste groups but would be a turn-off to the retro-kitchen taste group and an overkill for the wedding-registry group. For the first time, advertisers can see taste and make taste targeting a reality.

Rudimentary Taste Targeting Is Already Happening

Let's say that Ash has 30,000 followers on Instagram and Alex has 750,000. Who do you think is better at selecting relevant content for his audience? Intuitively, it seems that Alex is better because of the 30 times larger audience (the numbers seem to speak for themselves).

However, the ability to attract a large audience is not the same as the ability to engage a large audience. For example, a billboard on the highway has a large audience of tens of thousands of people per day. Yet the relevancy of the "Big Bob's Discount Mattress Emporium" billboard for drivers is exceptionally low. While the billboard company has the ability to capture a large audience by building a metal obelisk in people's line of sight, that's not the same as engagement.

The Internet equivalent of billboards is banner advertisements splashed up on websites everywhere (the ones that say such things as "learn this one, weird, belly-fat melting trick!"). Their engagement rates are measured, and we can get a pretty good sense of how low it is for mindless, scattershot advertising. Google (which displays its fair share of these advertisements) publishes its click-through rate for banner ads, which is defined as someone actually clicking (e.g., engaging) with the ad. From April 2016 to April 2017, Google's click-through rate for every banner advertisement globally was 0.19 percent.[27] This means that its average ad was shown 526 times before 1 person clicked (assuming it wasn't by accident or click fraud) and that there were 525 other times when people didn't see, ignored, or actively disregarded the message (e.g., "Ugh, I can't believe I have to keep looking at Big Bob's dumb billboard"). Banner advertising is not cool, *Mad Men*-esque advertising; it's the equivalent of a five-year-old yelling at the top of his lungs to look at his mortgage rates.

Engagement data exists for Ash's 30,000 followers and Alex's 750,000 followers on Instagram too. Will Alex's audience be more like a highway billboard, with most people actively ignoring posts, or will engagement be relatively high because, after all, they choose to follow Alex? HelloSociety studied this question using its own campaign performance data and, as it turns out, found that as audience sizes grow larger, engagement plummets. Specifically, Instagrammers with 35,000 or fewer followers have over 330 percent more engagement than those with over 750,000 followers.[28] And this measurement is from campaigns where a brand is specifically trying to raise engagement for its product. For example, an engagement may look something like the brand Lululemon approaching an Instagrammer and asking "will you take a photo of yourself wearing Lululemon while drinking a juice cleanse on a mountaintop doing sun salutation yoga poses"? And then HelloSociety tracks how well that content performs. The full numbers are given in Table 4.1.

First, it's worth pointing out that the opt-in nature of Instagram produces vastly superior engagement than the billboard-esque, scattershot-like banner advertisements across the web—even in the worst performing bracket (> 750,000). According to this research, it's 842 percent more effective (0.19 percent vs. 1.6 percent). So, the opt-in intentional nature of Instagram matters. And smaller audiences produce multiple times more engagement, shown by the 1.6 percent engagement in the largest audiences versus 5.3 percent engagement in the smallest. A similar study by the Influencer Marketing Hub found comparable trends by looking at over 100,000 profiles on Twitter. For example, a Twitter user with a smaller audience of fewer than 1,000 followers produced an engagement rate of 1.5 percent, whereas a Twitter user with a larger audience of more than 100,000 followers produced an engagement rate of 0.3 percent.[29] Like Instagram, as the audience size increased, engagement decreased.

Why is this the case? Why would smaller audiences produce more engagement than larger ones? Wouldn't those with the ability to attract a larger audience also have an outsize ability to engage that audience? After all, they did attract more people in the first place. Aren't those skills related?

In practice, there are many technical reasons why this could be the case. For example, some users are followed by automated bots (e.g., fake users),

Table 4.1   Engagement by audience size

Audience Size Range	Average Engagement Rate
< 35 K	5.3%
35k - 50k	2.5%
50k - 500k	2.3%
500k - 750k	1.5%
> 750k	1.6%

Source: Tori Stark, "Why Influencers with Smaller Audiences Are the Best for Your Brand's Holiday Campaign."

which distorts any study. Some users have a lot of followers because they were recommended programmatically by the platform as someone interesting to follow, the online equivalent of "bank error in your favor" and not exactly reflective of merit. But what it comes down to in the end is the least common denominator and whether a curator's selections appeal to a lot of people a little or a few people a lot. For example, there are things that lots of people have in common ("everyone" loves pizza), and there are things that fewer people have in common (like wanting quinoa every day). For the the pizza loving masses, they love to follow the user "Wood Oven Pizza" and see their artisanally crafted pies on Instagram. But the images only capture this large group's interest in food in the most general way; even among the throngs of pizza lovers, there's a wide range of preferences (e.g., the "Papa Johns is the end-all-be-all" group vs. the "I only eat the vegetarian, non-GMO pizza from worker-owned and -operated Cheeseboard Pizza in Berkeley, California" group). For the curators who focus on a niche such as quinoa, they're able to really engage the quinoa obsessed crowd with a parade of photos of quinoa salads, quinoa souffles, and recipes for the "best" quinoa dishes. This focus on quinoa, however, comes at the expense of engaging audiences who could be interested in almost anything else. Niche audiences may be more rabid, but they're also smaller; they find content they really care about, but because they really care about it, the odds that lots of people will care about it are lower. But as more and more curator's tap into their niches, more and more people will have the ability to find the content that really engages them. This trend doesn't bode well for traditional blanket, dumb advertising.

The End of Advertising

In the curated future, there will be little tolerance for dumb advertising. Banner advertisements will be derided as visual and cognitive pollution, and traditional advertising revenues will plummet. The *New York Times* will describe "objective advertising" as a crude and barbaric affront to our senses, much like we consider pop-up ads or spam to be today. In fact, the *New York Times* already does: "[W]hat's so bad about banners? For one, they have ruined the appearance and usability of the web, covering every available pixel of every page with clunky boxes of sponsorship. More than that, banner ads perverted the content itself. Because they are so ineffective, banner ads are sold at low prices for high volume. . . . This business model instilled the idea that page views were a paramount goal of the web."[30] With new ad-blocking tools that enable people to prevent ads from appearing in the first place, people have started taking matters into their own hands. By some measures, up to 30 percent of web visitors today block ads entirely.[31] And major web browsers, including Google's Chrome and Apple's Safari, have started blocking ads by default.

The curated future is one where trust between consumers and their curators reigns supreme. Audiences will look to curators to find the signal in the noise on their behalf. And it's a future where if marketers aren't approved by the curating class, they might not be heard at all. In short, it's the beginning of the end for traditional advertising and the start of a whole new way of buying products.

Advertisers Don't Pay the Cost of Producing Noise, Audiences Do

In the previous chapter, we saw that large audiences on Instagram have a much higher engagement rate (1.6 percent engagement) than audiences from banner advertising (0.19 percent). Yet despite the multiple improvements in engagement (almost 10 times better!), this still means that 98.4 percent of people—far and away the vast majority—don't give Instagram posts the time of day. The smaller audiences, in contrast, have a much higher engagement rate of 5.3 percent. So, why do advertisers like running campaigns with larger audiences when the smaller ones clearly show superior engagement?

It's because a small slice of a huge pie is much bigger than a large slice of a small pie. And, most critically, advertisers aren't charged for all of the advertisements that didn't engage anyone (e.g., the rest of the people in the much bigger pie that they annoyed in the process of engaging with their slice of it). Advertisers today aren't penalized for generating noise. This happens because in online advertising today, many of the most successful business models (such as Google's AdSense) only charge for performance. So, for example, an advertiser only pays Google when someone clicks on the ad, not just when Google shows the ad. With that arrangement, there's no downside to showing advertisements as frequently as possible, because only the interactions that happen (the engagement) get billed. With this billing arrangement, larger audiences become appealing because even with lower engagement rates, they still generate more clicks overall. For example, an audience size of 750,000 with a click-through rate of 1.5 percent provides engagement with 11,250 people (assuming a different person clicks each time). If you were to run the same campaign with a more engaged audience who clicks through at a rate of 5.3 percent but the audience size is smaller at 35,000 people, it would produce engagement with 1,855 people. So, even though the smaller audience size has over 3 times the engagement of the larger audience, the larger audience still reaches 600 percent more people (11,250 vs. 1,855)! For a business that's looking to sell more soap, reaching 600 percent more people from a large audience is compelling. And the fact that it took annoying 738,750 people to reach those 11,250—a full 22 times more annoyed people than the 33,145 annoyed from the smaller audience—simply doesn't matter; they didn't pay any more to produce that noise and annoy those people and, at the end of the day, produced more engagement.

Like a paper mill that dumps waste into the local river, advertisers today are able to externalize (dump) the costs of their campaigns on everyone in the form of noise. It's no wonder that this form of advertising is being blocked en masse by the world whenever there is a chance.

We're Tired of Ads Wasting Our Time

Overall, consumer's tolerance for mindless ads is decreasing, and their preferences for annoyance-free services are increasing. Rich Greenfield, managing director and analyst in the equity research team at BTIG, observes that "culturally, we're moving in the direction of no ads, or at least ad-lite. . . . Our tolerance for our time being 'wasted' by untargeted, annoying ads is dropping rapidly."[32] YouTube Music understands this as well; the company acknowledges that people find its ads annoying and then share their intentions to weaponize this annoyance to make people either quit YouTube or start paying. Lyor Cohen, YouTube's global head of music, says in a Bloomberg article that "There's a lot more people in our funnel that we can frustrate and seduce to become subscribers. . . . You're not going to be happy after you are jamming 'Stairway to Heaven' and you get an ad right after that."[33] The plan specifically is to target users who listen to the most music on YouTube and then give them proportionately more ads to try to annoy them into converting to the paid service. Cohen's annoy-them-till-they-quit-or-pay approach "will 'smoke out' people who can afford to pay for a subscription."

But just how much annoying advertising is necessary for people to either quit or pay? And does it make business sense overall? The Internet radio company Pandora conducted a study to answer this question. In this study, the company exposed 35 million people over a 21-month period to one of nine differing advertising frequency rates that ranged from high to low (high was nearly twice that of low). Unsurprisingly, as the company ran more ads, people listened to Pandora less. Specifically, "Serving one additional ad per hour resulted in a 2 percent decrease in average listening time and a 1.9 percent decrease in the number of days a user listened. The results were consistent across age groups, even though middle-aged users listen more hours than younger and older ones."[34] It's also true that people exposed to the most ads converted to the $4.99 per month paid service more often, with older people being twice as likely to pay than those under age 24. Greenfield compares these results to what's also happening with television: "'There's a reason why younger consumers are rapidly abandoning television,' which serves 18 minutes of ads per hour, Greenfield says. 'It's just a miserable experience with the ads.'" In the end, for every additional advertisement played per hour, the odds of a listener paying for the premium service increased 0.14 percent. However, the convert-through-annoyance approach comes at a cost; for each new subscriber, three others stopped using Pandora altogether, a loss of advertising revenue that doesn't offset the gains made from subscription fees. So, while playing more ads did increase the subscriber count, it hurt the company overall.

It's not just advertising and marketing that curators change; they change the way consumers buy as well. In the next chapter, we'll see how curation revolutionizes buying, starting with the fact that curators are the best salespeople.

CHAPTER FIVE

Curators Revolutionize Buying

Curators Are the Best Salespeople

Curators are not interested in your sales. That's what makes them such great salespeople. They are loyal to their passions, and your content is a means to their end. And you wouldn't want it any other way.

As it turns out, many people's passions are intimately tied to the content that enables them. Want to go camping? You might get pretty attached to your sleeping bag. Want a story? You might get pretty attached to a book. Love to run? You might develop serious preferences about running shoes. Curators catalyze passions, and passionate people open their wallets. Audiences never feel like they're being sold, because they're not; they're just people sharing passions, and sales are a by-product.

Curation is a form of content marketing whereby the curator indistinguishably weaves together free content, paid products, and brand-promoting imagery. A curated experience creates enjoyment, regardless of purchasing. As consumers, all we see are things we love.

Take home decor as an example. As the Internet generation starts buying homes and decorating them, they share photos of the decor on social media (like every other part of their lives). Social media acts as a source of inspiration as well (not to mention a point of comparison). Online, curators lead the charge, creating the rooms and designs of comparison. According to CNBC's review of the furniture market, "With everyone wanting a photo-worthy living space thanks to social media, bloggers and influencers are becoming in-demand tastemakers."[1] There's even a curation-centric start-up dedicated to home remodeling and design called Houzz, which is growing at an astronomical rate. Houzz's curation-centric model has powered it through raising over $600 million with a valuation of over $4 billion.[2]

Part of the reason sales increase with curation is that curators take the time to translate their specialized, subjective tastes for the benefit of others who often don't have the time to dedicate to discovering content. In short, the value of curation isn't just a curator's taste; it's a curator's ability to mediate between the time rich and the time poor.

Curation Mediates the Time Rich and the Time Poor

Do you have the time to keep up with and explore all the songs, books, TV, movies, games, apps, and products that interest you? Curators do. They spend enormous amounts of time evaluating content and handpicking selections. They act like content concierges, recommending things that might have otherwise taken months to discover, if ever, on your own. As a result, curation enables the time-poor masses to revive withered passions and indulge their interests; they get to spend less time looking for things and more time enjoying them.

The time commitment involved in curation isn't just required for content and products made for enjoyment; it directly impacts research in the sciences as well. In fields such as biology there is currently a crisis of curation, because despite a huge amount of research produced across the globe, much of it remains siloed and largely inaccessible to the researchers who could create life-changing discoveries from it. As reported in the science journal *Nature,* "curation is under-resourced," and "science funders and researchers need to recognize the time, resources, and effort required to curate open data."[3] To give an example, a researcher will make a discovery, write up his findings, and then publish the report in a journal. The idea is that the researcher's colleagues from around the world will hear about that research, access it, read the findings, and build upon the work (you know, science). Unfortunately, it's not that simple. Despite the paper being published somewhere, there's no guarantee that interested researchers will find it. As *Nature* describes it, these stores of knowledge "often restrict access to subscribers, curtailing opportunities for interoperability and collaboration."

But let's say that a researcher overcomes these restrictions, finds a relevant article, and decides to dig deeper. The next step would be to investigate the data used in the study to understand what happened. But again, due to a lack of curation, the supporting data is typically unavailable or stored in a such a way that a different laboratory can't make heads or tails of it. As a result, it can be prohibitively difficult to build from even the research you can find. Sabina Leonelli, the University of Exeter researcher who wrote the *Nature* article, observes that there is currently a lack of proper incentives to motivate someone to take on the expensive time commitments necessary for proper scientific curation. Specifically, "there is no reliable business model to finance the curation and maintenance of data repositories."[4] Despite the potentially life-changing discoveries that can be made by accelerating the sciences, in addition to the wealth of knowledge and expertise that exists in the field, when it comes to deciphering a way to employ curation effectively, researchers are in the dark ages.

In addition to the time rich and time poor, there is another related group that curation mediates: the passionately obsessed with the merely interested.

Curation Mediates the Passionately Obsessed and the Merely Interested

Like a Thanksgiving potluck dinner among friends, curation enables us to enjoy the best at the table. Curation in community enables everyone, whether they are time poor or time rich, to sustain more passions at a higher quality than they could alone—because even the most unconstrained curators are limited as to what they can explore. Curation in community lets us enjoy the content equivalent of Bob's amazing barbecue and Jane's incredible cakes while allowing us to focus on world-class lemonade. We get to connect to the most exemplary parts of many people (Figure 5.1): we don't all have to be as good as Bob at barbecue to enjoy his ribs.

It's the subjective equivalent of the classic economic theory comparative advantage. The theory says that if Ari is really good at raising chickens and Brook is really good at growing corn, then rather than both Ari and Brook raising chickens and growing corn, they should each specialize, produce chickens and corn at much higher rates, and trade the surplus for what they're not as good at. If they each embrace their comparative advantage, than Ari can focus on raising more chickens than anyone has ever seen, Brook can grow more corn than you can shake a cob at, and between the two they'll have more of each than before.

It's shocking that we haven't figured out how to translate this classic and powerful economic principle into a form that works for subjective discovery. While you may have hundreds of interests, you should specialize in discovering the latest and greatest and staying up-to-date in a select few and then trade those discoveries with other curators who discover the latest and

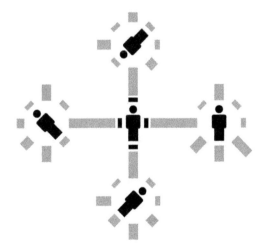

Figure 5.1 Curator's contribute their best, enabling everyone to discover better.

greatest in their interest (such as trading chickens for corn). Instead, however, we spend time looking across all our interests all the time. For example, if Tim wants to buy a special necklace for his girlfriend, he may find himself sorting through thousands of necklaces on Etsy until he can find the perfect design that matches both his tastes and his girlfriend's. Unfortunately, he may not have that kind of time or ability (because he's actually much better at discovering music), and as a result, he's unable to buy the necklace he wants, his girlfriend is unable to receive the gift, and the artisan who already made the perfect necklace in Wichita, Kansas, lost a sale. Nobody wins, because no one is able to exercise their comparative advantage. If Tim were able to exercise his speciality in a hypothetical curation market, he would spend his time discovering music for others and, with his discovery credits, trade them in for a link to the perfect necklace.

So why not? Why not establish a marketplace for subjective discovery? Part of the reason why comparative advantage works so well in economics is that the matching process is objective and easily performed; it's as simple as saying "You want corn? I have corn. Let's trade corn." If Ari wants to trade chickens for corn, he knows that he can go to the corn market and make the trade.

Unfortunately, it's not easy to match with subjective content. For example, if Ari wants to trade chickens for a necklace his wife likes, he can't easily match with the right necklace. It's not that there aren't artisans who will barter for jewelry; it's that Ari can't find the right necklace in the first place. While finding a necklace vendor matches the objective side of his need, it doesn't address the subjective side (e.g., these are all gold-chain necklaces; I wanted something in crystal that looks like a clump of grapes that remind me of the vineyards of my youth).

Classical economics takes the simplicity of objective matching for granted because it's so straightforward. It's simply not clear how you would structure a marketplace for subjective matching. But if you could, you'd be able to not just match the passionately obsessed with the merely interested; you'd be able to impact the global economy in much the way that current stock exchanges and marketplaces do.

Curators can mediate more than just people; they're capable of working across time, mediating the past with the present.

Curators Mediate the Past and the Present

In this eternal present, everything can be made contemporary.
Paul Ford, *Wired*, 2014

Curators are as comfortable in the past as they are in the present. If placing a piece of content in its historical or contemporary context helps curators convey their perspective, then they will—but the timeline is optional (Figure 5.2).

This makes curators largely immune to the 24-hour news cycle and to newness for its own sake. It frees them to seek quality whenever it occurred, whether it's in the archives of a blog, the back catalog of a publishing house, or the new releases.

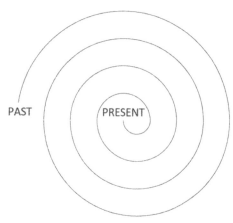

PAST   PRESENT

Having "everything" available on the Internet gives curators superpowers to mix the past with the present. Content that was once locked away in libraries and archives

Figure 5.2

has since been digitized and now streams freely at the tap of a smartphone. In Paul Ford's *Wired* article "Netflix and Google Books Are Blurring the Line between Past and Present," he observes that "Suddenly we find ourselves living in an online realm where the old is just as easy to consume as the new. We're approaching an odd sort of asymptote, as our past gets closer and closer to the present and the line separating our now from our then dissolves."[5]

Blurring the past with the present changes the competitive environment for contemporary creators. For example, creators used to have the competitive advantage of old things being difficult to discover and physically access (which basement archive is it in again?). But with music-streaming services such as YouTube and Spotify, it's just as easy for a curator to add Nat King Cole or Mariah Carey to a Christmas playlist. This means that for contemporary musicians who want a Christmas hit, they have to compete with the holiday gravitas of Bing Crosby, Frank Sinatra, and Louis Armstrong. It brings a new competitive meaning to the William Faulkner quote "The past is never dead. It's not even past." For writers, great novels across history are recommended as easily as new ones, making the competition for mind share not just against their contemporaries but also with every (remembered) writer before them. By highlighting work from the past and present, curators set this competition in motion.

The *New York Times* columnist Farhard Manjoo found that his two children, ages four and two, transitioned from listening to the popular pop of Maroon 5 and Michael Jackson to an obsession with the folk group Simon and Garfunkel from the 1960s. As a result of the curated playlists on Spotify, his children can easily bounce across handpicked songs from across time, brought together from a curator's point of view.

This phenomenon is not lost on Spotify. As Manjoo reports, "Spotify is betting that fixed musical genres will fade away."[6] Rather than listening to genre-specific things such as oldies or "electronic," Spotify is exploring genre and time-period agnostic approaches. The company's vice president of product says that "what we want to do is make Spotify more of a ritual." He describes it as forming a set of habits, such as listening to music while driving, working out, etc., and then Spotify will deliver the music (oftentimes curated) to program an entire day's worth of activity.

Sourcing Old and New

Curator Katherine Bragg worked at the design firm Roman and Williams, which made a name for itself for mixing old with new. This skill came partially from the founders first working on set designs in Hollywood. For example, when working on a set for, say, *Mad Men,* the firm would re-create the 1960s as accurately as possible. They'd meticulously select retro objects and, after putting them together, re-create the 1960s vibe.

Most people, however, don't want their home or office to feel like they're in a time capsule. As Bragg puts it, the trick is to mix old items with new to create a sense of timelessness. The goal is to give a nod to the past but make it contemporary with new meaning. Bragg shares the concept of a modern farmhouse as an example. It's cozy, casual, comfortable, and approachable but clearly not a re-creation of a 19th-century farmhouse with drafty windows, short ceilings, and an outhouse. The modern farmhouse mixes old with new, taking elements from the previous era to give the modern pieces—such as comfortable couches and king-size beds—context.

The ability to mediate the past and present requires knowledge of the past as well as the present. This knowledge gives curators another unique ability: an understanding of new content's significance in the here and now.

Curators Make Sense of the Here and Now

There will always be new things. The question is, do they deserve our attention? Curators have the answer. They do this by monitoring the relevant publishers, studios, blogs, YouTube pages, and brands in the cultural landscape. When something new comes out, their background knowledge allows them to contextualize it within a historical "family tree" of content and, like a good appraiser, assess its value (Figure 5.3). Their deep understanding of what's come before provides the perspective necessary to make sense of the here and now.

One of the most formalized examples of this is studying art history and launching a career in the professional art field. The art canon is so official, accepted, and relevant to the work in institutionalized art that universities around the world teach its history, and for museums, galleries, and auction houses hiring employees, it's viewed as table stakes for the job. For example,

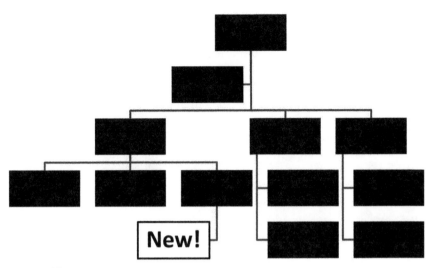

Figure 5.3

if you're working at an auction house and you need to fill a docket of big-ticket items for an upcoming auction, which pieces of art do you try to get on the block? Who currently owns them? For what price did they most recently sell? If you're not a big enough deal maker to connect with current owners, where might you find valuable pieces to bring into the auction house? All of these questions require intense knowledge of the art field. The same is true for museum curators as well. Not only do you need an opinion of which pieces to acquire, but you also need to know how much you're willing to pay. Whether the art is classic or modern, a deep understanding of its context is required to assess its value.

The same is true for any kind of curation, whether it's clothes, music, or GIFs of cute animals. In several ways, situating content in the here and now is when a curator is functionally closest to a critic and an appraiser. For example, if you're curating restaurants and you're trying a new sushi burrito establishment in the East Village, it's essential to have at a minimum an understanding of current sushi burrito restaurants in New York City and the Mexican and sushi restaurants in the area, a cursory knowledge of fusion food as a category, and a general familiarity with the East Village. It's from that knowledge base that you'd be able to act like a critic and make an assessment of this sushi burrito—whether the fish was fresh, the vegetables were well selected, and the value is high or low.

From the point of view of the appraiser, assessing the here and now is like watching an episode of *Antiques Roadshow*. Someone brings in what looks like a totally random antique bedside table, and with the appraiser's unparalleled knowledge of the past, he's able to determine that this is the table on which George Washington signed a purchase order for a horse and could fetch hundreds of thousands at auction.

A curator, who is already both critic and appraiser, brings even more to the table. Specifically, whereas the appraiser looks to identify the value and a critic looks to assess the rating, the curator assesses values and ratings for many audiences. For example, the curator may say that the sushi burrito is quirky and fun for the college set, blasphemous to the Mexican food diehards and sushi fans alike, a good value for Manhattan overall but a bad value for the East Village in particular, and, for the average amateur foodie, worth trying once for the novelty factor but overall lacking the substance to become a new category. When assessing George Washington's table, a curator may say that the Ikea crowd would donate it to the Salvation Army, the rustic modern people would pay up to $100 for it, the antique fans would bite up to $1,000 with the right story behind it, and the American history fanatics and museum crowd might pay hundreds of thousands for it.

Situating content in the here and now means that for a lot of things a lot of the time, curators realize that they're pretty "meh." But when something special comes along, a curator is likely one of the first to notice and, as a result, is in a position to tell the world that it's going to be a hit. In fact, if curators develop a reputation for finding hits, they can even develop the ability to establish hits.

Curators Establish Hits and Canonize Classics

Most of humanity's creative production has already been forgotten (Figure 5.4). Most content is birthed into obscurity and, even if it's noticed, quickly returns there. Take, for example, that the average American reads 17 books per year (according to the Pew Research Center).[7] These 17 books represent an infinitesimal 0.00001 percent of the Library of Congress's 158 million items.[8] If you're a librarian, a Barnes & Noble employee, a GoodReads user, or anyone curating a book collection or making book recommendations, you wield tremendous influence over the composition of a person's 17 yearly books. If you've ever influenced just one person to read just one book, you've

Figure 5.4

in fact grabbed 1 out of 17, or nearly 6 percent, of their book-reading mind share for the year. Your recommendation also shaped the livelihood and legacy of an author who, if it weren't for recommenders such as you, would almost inevitably slip into obscurity.

Advertising exists because businesses can't afford customers forgetting them. On average, a company spends 12 cents of every dollar it makes on marketing to make sure people keep buying their products.[9] But in an increasingly curated world, just buying ads isn't working like it used to. In fact, being known one year isn't enough anymore to be known the next year.

Let's look at an example from the music industry. In an article in Slate, Chris Molanphy did a back-of-the-envelope analysis on an artist's ability to have a top 10 hit the year after having a No. 1 hit. In 1984, 70 percent of No.1 hit artists had a follow-up with a top 10 hit the next year. In 1989, the figure increased to 79 percent. By 2010, 100 percent of artists with a No. 1 hit appeared in the top 10 the next year. But by 2013 the bottom dropped out, and there was a huge reversal; only 40 percent of No. 1 hit artists appeared in the top 10 the next year. Not only did listening habits change over this time frame, but as Molanphy notes, the way hits are measured changed too. Specifically, song popularity measurements started including music-streaming stats (not just the homogenous plays on the radio) and showed that as listeners, we're kind of flaky. As Molanphy observed, "what this data reveals about us isn't always pretty: It turns out we are fickle. Artist 'loyalty'? That's a 20th-century concept, friend."[10] It's also an editorial-style view of subjectivity and memory that divides the world into two camps—the ones that remember and the ones that don't. The goal then becomes to get as many people as possible into the "remember" category; from that point of view, it even makes sense to just advertise.

In a curated world, however, attention and memory fragments across many audiences. For example, a niche audience that's into straight-edge screamo music will never forget the song "Car Crash Hearts," while the punk guys have never heard of it. For fans of cupcakes, they may never forget when the Magnolia Bakery launched in New York City, kicking the cupcake craze into high gear—but for gluten-free fans, they heard about it and then promptly forgot. With memory distributed across a curated landscape, it means that a black and blue dress in most places would never have been known but on Twitter could become legendary, stirring a global debate on color perception and whether it's actually white and gold.[11]

With consumer memory and attention fragmented, it's more essential than ever to align with a curator to make your content known and remembered. One such tool a curator has is canonization. When a curator canonizes content, it becomes part of the official history of an interest and definitional of the interest itself. For example, there is a violin-teaching system called the Suzuki method that directs students to listen to songs before playing them from songbooks. To make this possible, Shinichi Suzuki curated pieces of music into a 10-volume curriculum. The second piece of music in the first volume is called "Lightly Row," which is Suzuki's arrangement of the 19th-century German folk song "Hänschen klein" ("Little Hans") by Franz Wiedemann. For most of the world, this song is unknown or, at most, a nursery rhyme. But for Suzuki's students it's legendary, because learning it required listening to it and practicing it thousands of times, searing the simple folk tune melody into every listener's mind. Suzuki's curation and canonization of "Lightly Row" made it unforgettable to generations of violin students and their parents.

But outside of this group, almost no one knows or cares about "Lightly Row." This is what it is to be canonized and remembered in a curated world; most content will be forgotten except that which is canonized. And not even "Lightly Row" was fully remembered, as the folk song has lyrics too! Suzuki only canonized the melody, leaving the lyrics about a young boy coming-of-age lost to the archives.

If you've ever wanted your work to be remembered for all time (or really just at all), consider allying with a curator. In the increasingly digitized and endlessly growing record of humanity, the curatorial process can canonize content and artists into rituals, stars, and hits, lifting tomorrow's legends and classics out of the bottomless sea of undiscovered and forgotten content.

The power to establish hits and canonize classics is significant, bringing with it heightened demand for curatorial talent. In fact, this demand has sparked a new kind of war for curators' talent.

CHAPTER SIX

The War for Curators

Building Curation Assets

If you are building a marketplace or a social platform, make sure to build curation into your model. It will make the service easier for everyone to navigate.

Fred Wilson, Union Square Ventures, 2011

Curators create incredible value: they organize content, lead trends, capture audiences, and consequently drive the bottom line. Businesses that foster and leverage curation assets steadily grow a competitive advantage that, once established, is hard to undermine, turning curation into a new business, core competency (Figure 6.1). Let's look at some examples.

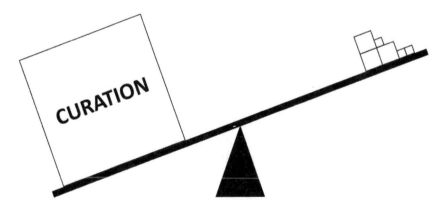

Figure 6.1

The curation platform Pinterest is projected to earn $3 billion in revenue in 2018 and has raised over $1.47 billion with a valuation of $12.3 billion.[1] It's rumored that the company may go public in 2019. For Pinterest, curation isn't just a core competency; it is the main competency. And Pinterest has been able to turn curation into a lucrative powerhouse. As a business, it is one giant curation asset with strong organizational knowledge about how to build an ecosystem of tools and opportunities that enables and rewards curators.

Moving on to Twitter, former Twitter CEO Dick Costolo says that curation is the future of the platform. Specifically, he says that "It's all about migrating a company from a world of being tech-centric, follow-based, reverse-chronologic-centric to a mix of that and curated, media-centric relevance-based content."[2] Today, it's a company learning the importance of building curation assets. Twitter started by launching a platform called Moments that features curated sets of tweets made by its team of in-house curators. Moments was then launched to the public for anyone to curate tweets starting in 2016.[3] With curation at the core of its strategy moving forward, Moments is now in a position to start building curation assets.

Google is building curation assets directly from its image search tool. Previously, searching images was just like searching the web; you'd punch in a query and get a result. Google's image search today, however, enables people to save images into collections, curating the images you discover.[4]

When eBay saw the business results of curation, the company jumped in head first. The company started with an acquisition of the online marketplace Bureau of Trade in 2013 for its ability to curate content and demonstrate that a curated approach has the ability to significantly drive up the selling price of items at auction.[5] The tech reporter Erin Griffith noted that "like many, many, commerce and social sites, eBay got a little Pinterest-y. The entire shoppable web is moving from text search and algorithm recommendations to browsable tiles of images curated by humans."[6] She describes eBay's new approach as "curated boutiques" where "images are the language of the web now and it takes a human to pick the good ones." In 2016 eBay hired Bradford Shellhammer, the founder of Fab.com (which raised over $330 million), to spearhead merchandising and curation.[7] Shellhammer says that in his role at eBay, he "will be focused on building new initiatives within the company, centered around telling stories, spotting trends, curating unique goods, and delighting customers."[8] By August 2016, the entire home page of eBay was populated with curated collections of boutiques of content as the company swallowed curation hook, line, and sinker.

The *New York Times* dove into curation in two big ways. The first is the acquisition of HelloSociety, the influencer marketing agency that got its start matching Pinterest influencers with brands. At the time of the acquisition, HelloSociety reported having more than 1,500 influencers in its network.[9]

New York Times CEO Mark Thompson said that the acquisition is about "the broader transformation of the way we think about digital advertising."[10] The second is the launch of NYT Cooking in 2014, which is a platform for the cooking team to not just publish recipes but also create a destination and community for cooking fans.[11] By 2017 the site grew to 10 million users and, based on the strength of the community and the content, the company decided to put it behind a $5 per month paywall. The value of the curated content and the curation community created another revenue stream from the *New York Times* in the hypercompetitive online recipe landscape.

The blogging platform Medium added the ability to curate collections in 2015 because there were too many new articles added every day to effectively discover quality content. When announcing the feature, the company said that "So many great stories are published every day on Medium—it's hard to keep up. . . . Today, we're making a change . . . to bring a bit of serendipity to our reading experience. . . . Our new home experience is powered by a feature called collections."[12] Medium has raised $132 million and was founded by several of Twitter's founders, including Biz Stone and Ev Williams.[13] For them curation is critical: "we believe that in order to create a great reading experience for humans, other humans should be part of that process."[14]

The largest music-streaming services in the world—Spotify, Apple Music, and Google Play Music—are some of the most vocal in the war to build curation assets as curated music experiences become standard. For Spotify and Google Play Music curation began in 2014 and for Apple Music in 2015. As of 2016, Spotify had 50 full-time curators on staff, Google Play Music had 20+ additional freelancers, and Apple Music had more than 12 curators in addition to freelancers.[15] The number of professionally curated playlists on the services total from 4,500 to tens of thousands. Some analysts estimate that across all music-streaming services, one out of every five songs played takes place inside a playlist, an amount that's only increasing. For Spotify in particular, a full 50 percent of its global base of 100 million users listen to curated playlists. From the point of view of Jay Frank, a senior vice president of global streaming marketing for Universal Music Group, curated playlists are reshaping the way people discover music. Frank comments that "all the signs point to playlists being the dominant mode of discovery in the near future." He points out that the trust found in another person is a large reason people appeal to playlists: "When it comes to trying to find something exciting and new, more people are going to want to go to trusted playlists."

Google moved into the curated music space with the acquisition of Songza in 2014 for an estimated $15 million.[16] This acquisition gave Google a staff of people who understand not only the art of curating playlists but also how to integrate them with technology. Google says that Songza "built a great service which uses contextual expert-curated playlists to give you the right music at the right time."

Apple Music grabbed curation assets by buying Beats Music for $3 billion, with $500 million attributed to the curated music service. Jimmy Iovine, a cofounder of Beats with Dr. Dre, discussed his curation strategy to the press, saying that "algorithms don't understand the subtlety and the mixing of genres. . . . So we hired the best people we know. Hired hundreds of them. . . . Curation is a big thing to us, and no one is going to be able to catch us or do it better. . . . Algorithms are great but they're very limited in what they can do as far as playing songs and playing a mood."[17] When Tim Cook, the CEO of Apple, experienced Beats Music playlists firsthand, he felt what Iovine was talking about: "So one night I'm sitting playing with theirs versus some others, and all of a sudden it dawns on me that when I listen to theirs for a while, I feel completely different. And the reason is that they recognized that human curation was important in the subscription service." And for Cook, this feeling was critical to acquiring Beats Music for $500 million: "[T]he sequencing of songs that you listen to affect how you feel. . . . It's hard to describe, but you know it when you feel it. So that night—I couldn't sleep that night! And I was thinking, 'We need to do this [the deal]."[18]

At around the same time, Apple also dipped its toes into curation by curating the app store for iPhones and iPads. The company started with the games section, adding the curated layer and de-emphasizing the algorithmic one. As Techcrunch reports, "Previously, developers relied on algorithmically generated sections highlighting new and trending titles. . . . In their place . . . are editorially curated lists instead. . . . Going forward, it seems that Apple is moving away from these algorithmically derived and more automated lists."[19]

In May 2017, the Apple App Store had around 2.2 million apps.[20] Yet despite the enormous selection, people are downloading fewer apps than ever, with 51 percent of people not downloading a single app in a month despite the fact that the app store received 500 million weekly visitors.[21] To encourage more downloads, in September 2017 Apple turned the app store into a predominantly curated experience, evolving as TechCrunch writes so that "the editorial voice now gets top billing, not the App Store charts and not even necessarily the new releases."[22]

Curation is big business, and some of the largest algorithmically driven companies in the world are embracing it. And while the content is diverse, one thing remains the same: building curation assets always requires people.

Curation Requires People

Automating curation with software is like interpreting poetry with a calculator; it just doesn't compute. Unlike a computer's ability to categorize objective measurements such as size and price, curation requires the subjectivity, emotions, creativity, and culture found in the human mind and

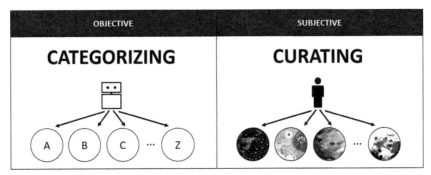

Figure 6.2 Computers are great at categorizing objective content. Only humans can curate subjective content.

heart—there are no algorithmic shortcuts. It's people-intensive and requires boots on the ground.

Now, this doesn't mean that there isn't a role for software in the curatorial process. One of the qualities of a good curator is monitoring the landscape, and social tools and keyword alerts are useful for surfacing new content. But in the seemingly limitless ways that software continues to make the world more efficient, curation will remain an exclusively human skill (Figure 6.2).

AI (artificial intelligence) is having an impact on the curation space, but not in the way you might think. AI at its core is advanced pattern matching. So, let's say that a human curates a collection of sad paintings and inside of the collection are pieces of art with predominantly deep purple, blue, and black coloration. AI could train on this collection of pictures and understand that these images have a certain range of dark hues in common. The software is then able to scan a library of other images (perhaps millions of them) and find other artworks that exist within the same range of dark colors. To the degree that dark colors make a painting sad, then AI can find sad paintings.

What's impressive about AI is that as essentially an advanced pattern-matching technology, it's capable of identifying almost any complex set of objective attributes such as colors and shapes. So, for those people who rely heavily on objective criteria to evaluate content (e.g., I like circles and bright colors!), AI will be helpful. But for everyone else who wants to feel delight, love, passion, and a whole range of subjective emotions, AI can't deliver.

Curation Powering Growth at VSCO

VSCO is an art and technology company that empowers people every-where to create, discover, and connect. Founded in 2011, its founders raised $70 million[23] in funding and in 2016 reported 30 million active users.[24] The company started when cofounders Greg Lutze and Joel Flory decided to create and sell professional-grade photo filter preset packs for use in picture-editing software such as Adobe Photoshop. It's the kind of thing where if you want a photo on your iPhone to look like it was shot on a Polaroid camera, you could apply the Polaroid 665 filter and voila, it looks retro.

Filter packs, however, turned out to spark Internet wildfire. While selling filters had some success, making them available in a free iPhone app was a smash hit. The VSCO photo filter app became Lutze and Flory's first major success, with over 1 million downloads in its first week.[25] And with those downloads came a rabid community of photographers taking millions of photos (with over 4 million photos tagged with "VSCO" on Instagram).

While originally formulated as a "freemium" strategy (which is essentially the Internet equivalent to the "first one's free" approach to marketing) for selling more filter packs, the VSCO founders quickly realized that they were onto something even bigger: a community. Instead of people taking photos and posting them to established social networks such as Instagram and Facebook, VSCO could become its own network. With a large install base already in place and a few small tweaks, they could shift their millions of users toward posting photos on VSCO itself.

But what kind of network would it be? It wouldn't explicitly be a social network, since we already have Facebook and Instagram. It wouldn't exactly be a professional networking site for creatives, since we already have Behance and Dribble. The VSCO founders decided that it would be a platform dedicated to self-expression. It would be about the photos, a "company empowering and inspiring people everywhere to create, discover, and connect."[26] They would explicitly avoid the mechanics of other social networks such as tallying one's followers, comments, and likes. They'd take inspiration from the museum gallery format and put the photos first.

The Curation Team Powers Strategic Growth

Standards do not set themselves, however, and it took a strategic, curatorial initiative to encourage the growing community to act more like the hard-core creative photographers. After all, if left to their own devices, the broader community could overwhelm the smaller set of professional curators with cat pictures! To set this standard, VSCO hired in-house curators to highlight what they see as the best photography from the community. One of the main outlets of this selection is the feed, a stream of photos prominently displayed to all visitors. Given the prominent attention that the feed gives photos, highlighting photos there accomplishes many goals. One goal is celebrating and directing current users toward VSCO's definition of good photography. It's worth pointing out here that despite calling them "curators," what they call curation is actually editorial. The VSCO curators essentially pick content that's either in or out of the feed, a binary decision that is the hallmark of an editorial process. If it were actually curation, the curators would have the ability to make multiple collections of different aesthetics (and not lump everything into the same feed). Now, if VSCO wanted to use curation proper to build the brand, this offers a lot of advantages. For example, the curators could explore the many different aesthetics that exist under the umbrella of quality professional photography rather than converging on an overall monolithic aesthetic that cannot appeal to everyone. They're likely running into this aesthetic ceiling right now as they continue to try to grow yet cannot appeal to audiences outside of the existing dominant aesthetic.

Curating the photos (editorial, really) accomplishes a second goal as well by modeling to new users what you can (and probably should) do with the VSCO app. This is accomplished first by example. All of VSCO's touch points, from the marketing of the app in the app store to its website to the onboarding experience of the app itself, is soaked in its curators' aesthetic. It's clear that while every other photo app may be for cat pictures, VSCO is for professional-level photography. A third goal that curating the photos accomplishes is building the VSCO brand as one that stands for a certain measure of discernment. The act of having curators selecting and featuring photos from the community sets the tone that this is a community of excellence and acknowledgment. For example, every time a photographer's photo is tagged as good by a curator, the photographer receives a notification informing of the accomplishment, further encouraging that good behavior.

Curators and AI as Gatekeepers between Creators and Brands

VSCO is exploring how to turn its community into a marketplace as well. VSCO Connect is the fledgling marketplace that matches brands with up-and-coming talent in the creative community. Brands and advertising agencies are interested in the VSCO community's photography because they're increasingly unable to keep up with the demands and rising standards of media quality required to be successful on social media. For example, brands find themselves in the position of paying more for photography assets (e.g., $40,000 to an agency for a set of photos), yet the results still aren't comparable to what influential creators post on Instagram;[27] they look inauthentic and too much like stiff stock photography.

This is where VSCO sells itself as a curated marketplace connecting brands with relevant, authentic photographers. For example, the energy bar company PowerBar was thrilled when it heard about the opportunity to connect with the right creators on VSCO. Jennifer Hirst, senior manager of social and digital marketing at PowerBar, runs a six-person internal creative team and felt the pain of traditional approaches to photography falling short on both price and quality. From her experience, "it is hard to find affordable talent. Consumers are getting more and more sophisticated in terms of visual aesthetic in the social and digital space, and the bar is continually set higher and higher for brands. . . . We can't get away with what we used to in terms of scrappy content. We need premium content that feels native and authentic to the user experience."[28] When exposed to the quality of content on VSCO, Hirst was blown away and became eager to find a way to partner. So, she dipped her toes in the water by developing a creative brief (a call for a certain style of photographs) for the VSCO Connect platform. For PowerBar's campaign, the team decided that "we are looking for a sense of joy in sports and camaraderie in the images. . . . We want there to be lightness and happiness to the story." With this aesthetic direction, VSCO's creative team took over, first looking to the machine learning system Ava (which is powered by the tags that curators made in the first place) to drum up results. The team then whittled down the results and provided Hirst a curated set of five photographers to choose from. Hirst made her selection, waited four weeks, and received the final photos from the photographers.

VSCO's marketplace is only possible with curation at the core. The curators drive value in previously unattainable ways, acting as an aesthetic intermediary between brands and creatives. For brands, they tap a diversity of authentic voices that were previously inaccessible at price points that were formerly unattainable. For photographers, they surface industry opportunities that were previously inaccessible, creating economic opportunities with top brands out of their photographic passion. As one reviewer of VSCO Connect puts it, the marketplace turns everyone's photos into a modern-day portfolio: "For young photographers interested in entering the professional creative industry, this is great news, as their VSCO platforms, which they use for creative/social purposes, could actually land them a gig. So, VSCO users, it may be time to up your photo game, because with VSCO Connect, your account may double as a resume."[29]

With everyone's account of photos now doubling as a résumé, it becomes clear that some photographers are better than others. The same is absolutely true of curation; not all curators are created equal.

Curators Are Not Created Equal

Many children can spout off about their favorite chocolate—but this doesn't mean that they know what they're talking about. It takes dedication to develop expertise in anything, including chocolate, and some people are better at it than others.

Take the two chocolate shops Delicious and Chocolate Empire, which compete in the Springfield Mall. In Delicious, Dan taste-tests and carefully organizes every variety. One section of his store has dark chocolates from Honduras, Mexico, and Argentina that are "intense and satisfying." In another section, he displays pieces filled with fruits, gingers, and spices. In a glass display cabinet are artisanal selections painted by French and Belgian artists. Dan dedicates an entire table to local chocolatiers who make limited batches, and on the wall are cases of chocolate-covered nuts, raisins, and pretzels drizzled in white, dark, and milk chocolates. Dan encourages sampling and loves to learn about your tastes in wine before making a recommendation.

Farther down the Spingfield Mall promenade, Chris at Chocolate Empire stocks Hershey, Nestle, and Cadbury brands with enough M&M's, KitKat's, and Snickers to fill a bomb shelter. There's a wall dedicated to M&M's with giant tubes of every color. Taste testing is not allowed, and most of the candy is sold by the pound. Chris carries a few international brands such as Lindt that occupy a small corner.

Now, it doesn't matter if you like mainstream or artisanal chocolate; in either case, Chris and Dan know more than you. They're among the best at what they do and, for example, if you like M&M's, there's almost no way you know more than Chris, who even tasted-tested the new raspberry flavor at the Candy Expo.

For every taste, there are skilled and unskilled curators (Figure 6.3). Because of the time, knowledge, and communication skills required to develop and share expertise, there aren't enough hours in the day to become an authority in everything. Some curators will always be more talented than others, and the businesses, marketplaces, and platforms that attract them will become better than others.

For example, some curators on Pinterest have hundreds of followers, whereas others have millions. What did the ones with millions do differently? Part of it can be attributed to being in the right place at the right time; some of these pinners report getting tons of followers for no reason, and some hypothesize that they were algorithmically recommended as people to follow to millions

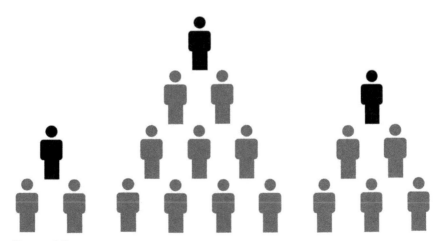

Figure 6.3

of new users when they registered. But that's not the reason for everyone. Part of it is that the content they curate is really good, and people want to see what's next.

Brenner, founder of the curator/influencer agency HelloSociety, noticed that certain curators exercised an outsize influence on product sales. For example, there was a curator on Pinterest with the handle "SF Girl by Bay" (her real name is Victoria), and after pinning a set of pencils from the store Uncovet, it sold out "like within an hour."[30] And this type of curator-spawned consumer mania isn't unique. Brenner could see in the data that "one pin would send thousands—sometimes tens of thousands—of unique visits, and it would result in sales that were much higher than they were from Facebook and Twitter, and sometimes even from search. It was crazy."[31] With the data showing this impact, Brenner saw a business opportunity to partner not just with curators in general but also the superstars in particular: "There are people who have massive audiences, so we take their huge reach and influence, and pair them with advertisers. We've now worked with almost a thousand brands, running campaigns through Pinterest."

In another example of a curator exerting outsize influence, Joanna Hawley is a 32-year-old Pinterest user with 3.7 million followers. She leveraged her curatorial influence to gain sponsorships to both remodel and decorate her new Seattle home. As CNBC reports, "Joanna Hawley is living a millennial's 'tiny home' dream, thanks to her Pinterest board."[32] In her publicly curated remodeling project, she was able to corral retailers including Pottery Barn, CB2, The Modern, and The Mine, which aided with furniture, draperies, and paint. In exchange for curating their products onto her Pinterest boards, these brands "ended up paying for a huge part of her remodel and outfitting."

With some curators able to drive more impact than others, it's increasingly important for a business to attract curators and have them active on their platform and with their content. Next, we'll learn about how to set curator bait and attract curators in the first place.

Curator Bait

Content to a curator is like coal to a steam engine: content keeps the curator running. But while curators go where the content goes, content doesn't go everywhere. Businesses with locked-down content that is exclusive or unique more easily attract curators who can't go anywhere else to find it. For example, where does an ambitious DJ make playlists of new and unique music when services such as Spotify, Rdio, and Apple Beats have the same licensed catalogs of songs from the same record companies? They head to SoundCloud, where artists, signed or unsigned, can upload their songs. SoundCloud's collection of unique content gives them an advantage in attracting curatorial talent.

UNIQUE   QUALITY

Figure 6.4

A second way to attract curators is with high-quality content (Figure 6.4). For example, while YouTube has the most videos on the Internet, as it turns out independent filmmakers often embrace Vimeo. This concentration of high-quality content attracts curators to Vimeo despite and partially because of its smaller size.

A third way to attract curators is to provide tooling that caters to their needs. Examples include the ability to search for content, filter by category, and make lists. This may seem obvious, but many digital destinations still lack these basic functionalities. For interior designer Katherine Bragg, the experience between a destination that considers 21st-century curators and those that don't is vast. In fact, she's almost given up on stores that haven't kept up with digital conventions (which are many in the interior design industry). For example, physical vendors don't have searchable websites, and compared to the ones that do, Bragg just doesn't have time for physical vendors anymore. If it's not searchable by keyword or filterable by color or size, she wants to pull her hair out. And this comes from an interior design professional who's both compensated for this work and familiar with pre-Internet customs. Imagine how much of a nonstarter this situation is for millenials; they'd look at you like you're an alien. It becomes clear that even after a business attracts curators, the curators have requirements as well.

Curators Have Requirements

The curating class has specific requirements and expectations. Platforms and businesses that build to these requirements can start to attract them. These requirements include the following items:

- Is it easy and intuitive to start curating? If not, it probably won't happen!
- Does the final collection look beautiful? If it doesn't, why would a curator feel proud or motivated to build or share the collection?
- Is there a community? If curators don't feel appreciated or noticed, they will likely go to a community where they are.
- Is expertise recognized? If a world-class curator is treated the same as a casual user, the world-class curator may jump to a platform where her or his expertise is recognized.

- Is there compensation? In the broadest sense, what does a curator get by curating? Platforms that reward the curator class will excel at attracting those people.

One of the best ways to understand the requirements and preferences of a curator is to do some curation yourself. In the next chapter, we'll investigate the process of curation itself. You'll learn the principles of curation and practical techniques to start curating today. If you're a curating novice, you'll learn enough to get your feet wet. And if you've a curating expert, you'll learn how to hone your craft.

PART 3

How to Curate

Introduction to Part III

Everyone Is a Curator

Good news. You're already a curator. When you build a playlist of songs to work, dance, or relax to, you curate music. When you choose your outfits, you're curating clothing. When you plan a meal, you're curating a set of dishes. Curating is so common that specific kinds of curated collections have their own words to describe them, such as "outfits" (clothing), "anthologies" (stories/poems), "curriculums" (research), "libraries" (media), "decor" (furnishings), "galleries" (art/images), "playlists" (music), "meals" (food), "tastings" (wine), "channels" (video), "stations" (radio), "festivals" (film/vendors), "exhibits" (artifacts), "swatches" (colors), and even "teams" (people).

Good curation, however, doesn't happen by accident. It's also not a formula. It's part craft and creativity. Whether your goals are marketing, personal branding, recreation, or enrichment, the principles of curation taught in the next chapters will set you on your way to becoming a master of the craft.

CHAPTER SEVEN

Curation Concepts

Interconnectivity

Ice cream, whipped cream, and chopped walnuts make a sundae. Chopped walnuts, arugula, and hard-boiled eggs make a salad. Arugula, ice cream, and hard-boiled eggs make us vomit. Like these ingredients, each piece of content in a collection relates to and interacts with every other piece (Figure 7.1). And each addition, or subtraction, alters the context of the collection as well.

Good curators select new content cautiously because of this interconnectivity. Like a chef debating the use of cayenne pepper in a new pasta recipe, it's not a question of whether cayenne pepper is good or not. It's a question of how adding or withholding cayenne pepper changes the dish.

Leslie, the creator of Catch My Party (with over 770,000 followers on Pinterest), separates her professional brand from her personal aesthetic due to the effects of interconnectivity in a collection. She does this because as it turns out, her professional brand and personal aesthetic are at odds with one another. On the one hand, she likes the look of over-the-top welcoming parties; they're bright, happy, and abundant. Her

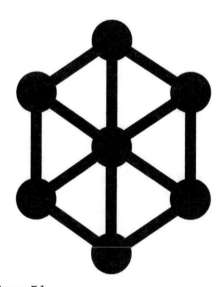

Figure 7.1

personal style, however, leans toward minimalism. As she describes the division, "I have two Pinterest styles. One is for our party boards. For those I like photos that are beautiful and vibrant, with lots of details, and a little decadence. Give me a photo of a gorgeous dessert table, filled to the brim with desserts, and I'm delighted. For my personal boards, I like beautiful photos that are more modern and stark, lots of blank space. It's a funny dichotomy."[1] In order to curate well, she embraces the interconnectivity of each of her aesthetics by keeping them separate.

Interconnectivity and Interior Design

Katherine Bragg is a nationally recognized interior and product designer who's curated for luxury merchandisers such as Tiffany & Co. and Hollywood stars (including Ben Stiller and Gwyneth Paltrow, whom she affectionately calls "Gwenny"). Interior design is the profession dedicated to curating the items inside residential and commercial spaces. An interior designer often selects everything from the paint on the walls to the coffee tables (including the coffee-table books on them).

While Bragg worked with the New York–based design firm Roman and Williams, the firm won the Smithsonian Design Museum's Cooper Hewitt National Design Award for interior design, an award that honors lasting achievement in American design. The award was first launched at the White House in 2000 as part of the White House Millennium Council, and the awards are, "bestowed in recognition of excellence, innovation, and enhancement of the quality of life" (you know you're a star curator when the Smithsonian invites you to the White House for your curation skills and "lasting achievement in American design").[2]

In Situ

Context is super important. Otherwise, you lose meaning.

Katherine Bragg

The Latin phrase "in situ" literally means "in its original place or position," and it's a huge word in interior design. In Bragg's current work, she refuses to present individual pieces to clients. By doing so, the item would exist out of context and lack the necessary framing to give it its full meaning. She avoids bringing items out one-by-one to clients because she finds that they get sidetracked without seeing the "whole picture."

In fact, Bragg goes as far as not presenting a space until all of the items are selected. How is this possible, given that you need to sell a client on a curatorial vision before actually buying and curating the client's space? 3D modeling. In order to present the context, Bragg re-creates the rooms in 3D, creates all the objects she'd like to acquire in 3D as well, and then meticulously arranges them in the 3D environment to fully prototype her curatorial vision. It's only within a fully contextualized in situ environment that she presents her vision to clients.

Interconnectivity and Multiple Audiences

Curators often make collections with several audiences in mind. For example, when Bragg designs a room, she'll often consider four audiences simultaneously: the client, herself, future clients, and her peers. To begin with, it's essential for her to delight today's client because, like all businesses, the client is the paying customer. This is true for superstar curators contracting with brands on social media as well, because if the sponsor isn't happy, it's unlikely that the sponsor will work with that curator again. Next, satisfying herself is a top priority, because the client is typically paying for her expert taste; if Bragg's not satisfied with the outcome, then the client isn't receiving the full value of working with a top curator. This is true for social media curators as well; a brand isn't working with the curator to have the curator work against her own taste; the brand wants the curator (and, by extension, the brand's audience) to be thrilled with the outcome so the brand can be a part of it. The third audience that Bragg has in mind is future clients. It's essential to curate with the next client in mind, because today's project becomes the calling card for tomorrow's customer. As a result, if Bragg doesn't like the direction of today's project, it likely won't be helpful in generating new projects that she will like. For example, the luxury loft–owning clientele in New York City's Tribeca and San Francisco's South of Market district are unlikely to be impressed by the portfolio of a budget motel curator even if the projects were of amazing quality given the constraints. The final audience is her peers in the industry. Not only does impressing one's peers help establish a reputation and cultivate new engagements, but it also leads to being published in periodicals and magazines that further establish one's reputation and professional sphere of influence.

Curating for these four audiences can be quite irritating to outright destructive when a client buys something for a project or insists that a specific piece be included. Without knowledge of a collection's interconnectivity, people can be surprised that by just adding one thing, the course of the entire project can change. While customers may think they're getting what they want to some degree (such as the inclusion of their favorite couch), they're losing out on the curator's judgment and vision. Furthermore, the curator is now more likely to hide the fact that they worked together (and may choose not to work together again) because the project didn't add to a portfolio that could attract future clients or impress industry peers. In practice, though, negotiations occur and exceptions are made. For example, Bragg relented when Gwyneth Paltrow felt strongly about including a particular sofa and modified her design to accommodate it.

Longevity

Tweets on Twitter and messages on Facebook aren't interconnected. Like most Web 2.0 social media, they are linear, with tweets appearing one after another and Facebook messages replying back and forth. As a result, to stop messaging on these platforms is akin to silence. It's like going to a party and sitting alone in the corner: you might as well have not shown up.

To promote products, content, and events on Twitter and Facebook, you have to keep the conversation going. And to avoid the silent corner, people end up running on a never-ending treadmill of comments, observations, current events, and status updates. The demands are so pronounced that an entire industry of tools were spawned with firms such as Hootsuite, providing scheduling and automation solutions for the beleaguered social media professional.

When content is interconnected, however, it's transformed from a conversation into a destination. If you've ever felt overwhelmed by social media, it may be because it's a lot like planting grass one blade at a time; sure, sometimes it spreads like a weed, but in social media most of the time you end up with a small withered patch of updates on your profile. One study showed that of 1.6 million social posts on Twitter, Facebook, and Google+, 99 percent of them created "little to no engagement at all."[3] Ninety-nine percent! So, most of social media is a lot of sound and fury signifying nothing—a conversation no one is having with you.

Now let's look at curation. It's not a one-way conversation; it's a destination. For example, consider the chef behind the Cronut (a croissant donut). Dominique Ansel doesn't need to develop entirely new recipes every day at the speeds and demands that Twitter would require. The Cronut has longevity, and people will talk about his sugary, interconnected contribution of croissant, donut, and oil for years to come. It's the same when DJ Tiesto goes on tour or the furniture curators exhibit at the Metropolitan Museum of Art: their interconnected collections serve as substantive attractions and resources that people talk about on social platforms. Museum collections tour around the world so that more people can partake. This makes a curated collection a lot like a great tree in a meadow: the grass and weeds of social media grow and die around it while it continues to grow and flourish. Online publishers are following suit, finding ways to transform once ephemeral content into more evergreen content. For example, *New York Magazine* used Facebook to repost a nine-month-old article about a New York City–based writer leaving the city. Despite its age, it ended up becoming *New York Magazine*'s second most read story, with 76,000 views.[4] The magazine's observation was that the Facebook audience grew three times since the article was originally published, meaning that 80 percent of that audience wasn't around when it was originally published.

All of this highlights the importance of timeliness in finding content. While smart curation can turn content that started a conversation into a persisting destination, finding great content first is powerful as well. In the next section, we'll dive deeper into timely content curation and its value.

Timeliness

Investors profit when they see value before others. Editors sell more books when they sign up-and-coming authors before their peers. Art dealers succeed when they discover artists before they break; in any industry, it pays to know what's next.

The same is true for curation. Whether it's for audiences large or small, curators gain influence when they develop a reputation for leading trends. At its most essential, finding what's next is about discovering likable content before other people (Figure 7.2). It's like a batting average whereby instead of hitting balls, you discover good things early. And curators often do just that.

Markets for Subjectivity

Recognizing value is an essential moneymaking skill. For example, skilled value spotters in finance flock to the stock market in droves; these talented investors identify valuable companies before others and profit when others figure it out later and drive up the price. The higher-priced stock more accurately reflects the new consensus of the company's value and, as a result, compensates the skilled investor.

The marketplace compensates curators too. The skilled curator can consistently spot undervalued objects—such as an artwork, an unsigned artist or writer, or a cool hat—and profit from future price increases. In the case of discovering an up-and-coming painter, the profit may be financial when buying a painting for a low price and then selling when it's high. In the case of discovering a cool hat the profit may be social, with lots of compliments from friends or new followers on Instagram (which could potentially convert into influence and sponsorships).

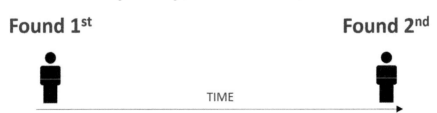

Figure 7.2

While some of the most famous markets are stock exchanges such as the New York Stock Exchange, there also exist markets to trade ideas. They're called idea markets, and some of them, such as the Iowa Electronic Markets, even receive prime-time news coverage.[5] For example, reporters quote the Iowa Electronic Markets during presidential elections as an alternative to traditional polling. The Iowa Electronic Markets works when people buy and sell shares in presidential candidates who run for office. Collectively, the total knowledge of buyers and sellers is often more accurate than traditional polls; for example, the Iowa Electronic Markets has predicted presidential election outcomes more accurately, 75 percent of the time, than traditional polls since 1988.[6]

Idea markets can exist for anything that people want to trade, including subjective cultural objects such as music, fashion, and movies. For example, the Hollywood Stock Exchange (HSX) is an idea market for movies and movie stars. When people sign up, they receive 2 million Hollywood Dollars to start buying or selling movies and actors. If someone thinks that *Avengers 12* will be a bigger hit than people expect, they buy shares. If they think Kevin Spacey has peaked, they short Spacey stock and wait for the price to fall. For traders skilled at identifying movies and actors on the rise or on their way out, they profit and climb HSX's internal rankings of "rich" Hollywood insiders.

Market prices on the HSX are accurate as well. As the data journalism site FiveThirtyEight reported during Oscar season, "The betting market basically nailed it. All eight films nominated were among the top nine favorites on the HSX. . . . The HSX also nailed the best actor nominations."[7] FiveThirtyEight also observe that for something as subjective as film awards, the HSX if pretty effective at capturing subjective opinions: "Monitoring betting markets has been one of the more consistent ways to get inside the Academy's head . . . to see who's putting their (fake) money where their mouth is." The Harvard Business School reports on the HSX's accuracy as well, writing that "the Hollywood Stock Exchange has forecast Oscar winners more effectively than even the most seasoned media critics seven years running."[8]

In 2001, the financial firm Cantor Fitzgerald purchased the HSX with the ambition of turning it into a real financial futures market (turning Hollywood Dollars into U.S. dollars). The logic went that while today you can buy futures in grain, precious metals, and meat, Cantor Fitzgerald would make it possible to also buy futures in Peter Jackson's *Lord of the Rings*. However, four months after acquiring the HSX, 658 of Cantor Fitzgerald's employees died in the World Trade Center attacks, delaying the development of the idea for seven years. By the time the company brought the proposal to the congressional subcommittee on agriculture in 2008 for approval, the go-go world of financial engineering had changed, and it was the start of the great recession. While Cantor Fitzgerald pitched a real HSX as a form of economic stimulus that would make Hollywood investing more predictable and investor friendly, the Hollywood industry pushed back in force; movie studios, agencies, and guilds banded together into an anti–movie-trading coalition and successfully lobbied Congress to outlaw movie futures. The movie industry argued that such a market would add an "aura of financial authenticity to gossip" and that it would be "more of a wild card then a stabilizing force."[9] Others argued that the industry was terrified of financial accountability.

Despite not evolving into a real financial market, the HSX as a game powerfully demonstrates the timeliness of trend hunters. The market-based approach, however, comes with limitations. A large one is that a market is not a curatorial approach to measuring subjectivity. The idea that a singular market price is appropriate to measure the value of a film or anything else is classic editorial-style thinking that forces everything to be either in or out or to be a buy or sell. While the markets efficiently summarize everyone's opinion into a single value (it's worth $99!), tracking these values also creates perverse incentives such as justifying buying stock in Justin Bieber, not because you like his art but because you know that people in aggregate like him and that his price will rise, or choosing not to sign an author you really like, not because you don't think it's good but because you're not sure it will sell enough in aggregate to hit your numbers. In contrast, a curatorial approach to a marketplace could, for example, assign multiple prices to content to reflect the true underlying value that varying audiences ascribe to it. For example, a film may have a 50 percent score on the review site Rotten Tomatoes (reflecting a singular editorial view) that actually decomposes into two groups with one that rates it 100 percent and another that rates it 0 percent (the curatorial reality). While the final editorial score of 50 percent is mathematically correct, it hides the fact that some people loved it and others hated it; not a single person actually felt on the fence with a score of 50 percent. Market-based models have yet to evolve to unlock the power and diversity that curation brings to valuing content and identifying trends.

The ability to price content correctly and discover value early leads us to our next curation concept: dependability. It's not enough to find something good once. A profitable curator must find good things over and over again.

Dependability

Be the Signal

A museum curator celebrates the 565th birthday of Leonardo Da Vinci by developing a Renaissance exhibit but includes several framed Garfield cartoons. A DJ performs at a wedding reception but includes songs by Metallica.

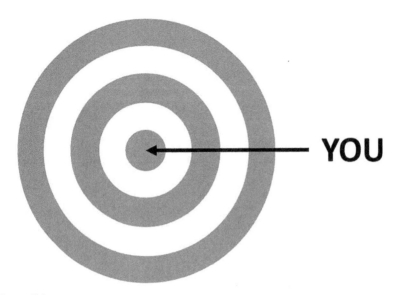

Figure 7.3

When people talk about the signal and the noise, the noise can be like these curators who don't stay on point.

Curators have the opportunity to be the signal for others. Being the signal means staying focused on a theme (Figure 7.3). It also means exercising self-control so that even if you do see a fascinating connection between Garfield and the *Mona Lisa,* you don't use an exhibit advertised as *The Renaissance* to explore it.

Learn How to Say "No"

Harvard admission officers don't say "yes" to every high school valedictorian with perfect SAT scores. Successful investors don't say "yes" to every business plan that crosses their desk. Editors at *Wired* magazine don't say "yes" to every article pitched to them. Good curators selectively say "yes" to exceptional things and "no" to most things. This is often counterintuitive on the social web, where "more" equates to "better" and silence feels like nonexistence. To curate is to realize that the only way to exercise expertise is to say "no." It's only by saying "no" that you can become the signal and earn a reputation as a dependable source.

Museum curators are no strangers to saying no—not just to potential work they could acquire but also to people looking to donate pieces to the museum. It's so common in their occupation that the *Wall Street Journal* looked into the many ways curators say to donors "no thanks." It's especially critical for museum curators to say "no" well, because donations can constitute 90 percent or more of their collection, and burning bridges is not an acceptable option. Saying "no" is also a common response, because a large portion of donations are not welcome, which can be for many reasons including it's too similar to items already in the collection, it's in poor condition, it's not exactly what the owner hopes it is, it comes with too many strings attached, it has an ambiguous ownership history ("Oh, so your grandfather acquired this painting during the war? I see."), or it may not be aligned to the mission of the museum. For example, Graham Beal, director of the Detroit Institute of Arts, had a donor seek to contribute a cracked mirror because of how beautifully it had cracked in the woods. Beal had to inform this well-meaning donor that this kind of object isn't in line with the mission of the museum, as "the point of an art museum is that everything here is made by hand."[10] Other data points show that the Virginia Museum of Fine Arts in Richmond rejects around one-third of donated pieces, while the Houston Museum of Fine Arts rejects around 9 out of 10 donated pieces. Peter Marzio, the director of the Houston Museum of Fine Arts, says that with so many inbound options, "It's easy to let your standards drop." But it remains critical to learn how to say "no" so that you're favorably positioned for the moment when you want to say "yes."

Curators Don't Make It about Themselves

Leslie, founder of Catch My Party, knows that her audience is "really busy moms." With that insight into her audience, she thought at one point that maybe other moms would be interested in stories about her children. After all, she's a really busy mom too, and wouldn't that make the content more personal, more authentic even? She was surprised at what she found after sharing about her own kids: "yesterday I shared a really quick story about my daughter's first day of fourth grade. But the truth of the matter is, people don't care that much about that."[11]

Leslie discovered that her audience didn't care about her personally; rather, they were interested in her well-curated party content. This is true for most curators. Unless you're a celebrity and your lifestyle is itself content— Who are you dating? What are you wearing? Where did you vacation? Do you have kids, and how was your daughter's first day of fourth grade?—then it's best to focus on the things for which your audience follows you. As Leslie puts it, "What I try to share are things that I find in the world that I think are cool. Because if I think it's cool maybe you'll think it's cool. I'm always thinking in terms of how can I provide value and not just make it a platform all about me."[12] In short, you need to be dependable and say "no" to a lot of things you might think are interesting—including stories about your kids.

Curating as a Herd

If there were ever a place where you'd think curators would have the right incentives to curate dependability, it would be investors curating portfolios of stocks worth billions of dollars. Yet even in this context, many investors choose to curate mindlessly. The financial community calls this behavior "herding," a term that can be applied to curators who decide to make decisions according to the masses rather than by their own judgment. For example, there was a time when "everyone" thought that videos of otters holding hands were adorable; jumping on the otter train at that point would have been an example of joining the herd. And there was a time when having an asymmetrical haircut would have been seen as weird and deviant—until all of a sudden it wasn't. Spotting that fashion opportunity when it was nascent would be thinking, in finance lingo, like a contrarian.

While running my curation analytics start-up Curalytics, I wanted to see if it was possible to find curators who herd and the contrarians who think independently among professional investors. The idea came from my dad, who observed that investors operate a lot like curators because they formulate opinions about which stocks are worth holding and build (e.g., curate) portfolios. While all investors try to invest as rationally as possible, the markets present a lot of imperfect information, making judgment calls necessary and producing varying opinions. Given this subjectivity, would it be possible to discover just how prevalent herding versus contrarian curating behavior is among institutional investors?

Answering this question would first require data on the portfolios of professional investors (normally closely guarded secrets). As it turns out, however, the Securities and Exchange Commission (SEC), the regulatory body that enforces laws affecting the stock markets, has a law that requires investors with portfolios valued at more than $100 million to disclose their portfolio to not just the SEC but also the public. Every quarter, the SEC collects the contents of more than 3,100 investment portfolios on form 13F, which is then published publicly on the SEC's FTP server. In other words, the government forces the largest investors to digitize the contents of their portfolios and dump it onto a computer where anyone can download and view it.

But the SEC doesn't make it easy. Like most data science projects, preparing the data for analysis requires a lot of up-front data-munging work. In this case, it required deciphering form 13F's ludicrous file structure (who encodes their data in XML anymore?!), downloading the relevant portfolio information (in this case, the portfolios of stocks from the fourth quarter of 2014), figuring out a way to parse the files and put the data in the format I needed, and then finally running the analysis itself.

A key decision while running the analysis is defining how similar two portfolios need to be to be considered similar. Is 10 percent similar enough, or is only 90 percent similar enough? For this analysis, I defined similarity as any portfolio that contains 50 percent or greater of the same stocks. So, for example, if Bob invested in Apple, IBM, and Alphabet and Ash invested in Apple, IBM, and Disney, then Bob's and Ash's 66 percent commonality would make them similar. The results of the study (first published by the investment news and analysis publishers ThinkAdvisor) reveals that out of the 3,100 portfolios that filed form 13F, 593 overlap (19 percent) in similarity, with at least 1 other portfolio with an average group of similar portfolios consisting of 17.6 funds; the largest group contained 46 funds.[13] This means that not only do 19 percent of some of the largest portfolios of stocks in the world herd together with at least 1 other fund, but 46 of them herd together as a single group as well.

In the investment community, it's no secret that some investors think alike. And in this case, we can put a number to it: 19 percent (about one in five) of America's largest investors herd together. This is shocking, because institutional investors market themselves as having unique perspectives and proprietary research that gives them an edge in the marketplace; this is, after all, why you invest with them (and why they charge their fees). If you just wanted to buy what everyone else was buying, you could do that yourself. Yet even among this group, there are those who do more discovery work than others, some who take more risks by curating outside the mainstream, and others who, whether they know it or not, curate with the herd.

In your own curation, do you curate like a contrarian and experience outsize profit, or do you curate with the herd and fall with everyone else? One way to tell is to see how your curation follows these principles. These principles, covered in the next chapter, will equip you to diagnose your own approach to curation and turn yourself into the Warren Buffett of your own taste. Buckle up: you're about to learn how curation really gets done.

CHAPTER EIGHT

Curation Principles

Discovery is seeing what everybody else has seen, and thinking what nobody else has thought.

Albert Szent-Gyorgyi

The real voyage of discovery consists not in seeking new landscapes, but in having new eyes.

Marcel Proust

Bottom-Up Curation and the Classification Rule

Buying a painting and figuring out which room to hang it in later is an example of curating from the bottom up. It's an inductive approach that begins with a general impression such as "That painting makes me hungry!" and creates context for it later such as "It would look great in my kitchen!"

If you've ever "liked" something on Facebook, "favorited" a tweet on Twitter, or "thumb-upped" a video on YouTube, then you've practiced the first part of bottom-up curation—thinking that something is worthy.[1] This first step is called the classification rule and can be as straightforward as having a feeling about something. In contrast, liking stamps because they let you mail letters or coins because they let you buy things lacks the necessary subjective or aesthetic appreciation to be curation. There has to be something more than an object's utility, such as a coin's historical significance or a stamp's aesthetic appeal.

Once you've determined that a stamp is beautiful or that a painting makes you hungry, then you can perform the second half of bottom-up curation: include it in a broader theme (Figure 8.1). For example, a painting might join the theme "Art for the Appetite," or a stamp might join the theme "Tiny

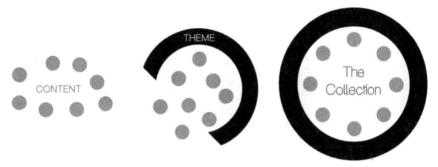

Figure 8.1

Pictures of Hamburgers." Regardless of what the theme is, developing it after thinking that something is worthy makes it curation from the bottom up.

Top-Down Curation and the Reframing Rule

Agreeing to be a bridesmaid and figuring out the dress and shoes later is an example of curating from the top down. It's a deductive approach that begins with a theme such as "purple bridesmaids dresses on the beach" and actually finds the purple sundress, midheel sandals, and seashell necklace later.

If you've ever had to dress a certain way for work or pick out a restaurant your in-laws will like, then you've practiced the first part of top-down curation—choosing a theme.[2] This first step is called the reframing rule and can be as straightforward as having a requirement or a need. In contrast, a requirement that is completely objective, such as the need for a sundress in size medium, lacks the necessary subjective and aesthetic requirements that the reframing rule requires. There has to be something more than a purely objective requirement, such as the need for a flattering sundress.

Once you've determined that you need a predominantly purple flattering outfit for the beach, then you can perform the second half of top-down curation: find the specific dress, sandals, and accessories (Figure 8.2). Regardless of what the specific outfit ends up being, that the specifics are chosen after determining the theme makes it curation from the top down.

When working on interior design projects, Katherine Bragg typically works from the top down. For example, she'll have an idea in mind and then find objects that fit within that idea (and the project's budget). But sometimes she works from the bottom up as well. For Gwyneth Paltrow, one engagement started with a specific wallpaper design and an Indian swing. Those two items drove the rest of the space.

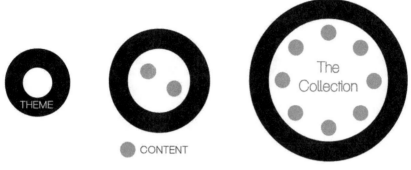

Figure 8.2

The Discrimination Rule

A librarian fills a bookshelf with copies of the same book. A photographer's portfolio contains identical photos. A DJ performs at a festival and plays the same song twice in a row. In each of these examples, a curator breaks the discrimination rule.

Content must be considered different from, at a minimum, the curator's point of view to be considered curation.[3] A collection that repeats content without reason dilutes the collection's theme and, if repeated enough, ceases to be curation at all. It's like serving a five-course meal where every course is coleslaw: it doesn't make any sense.

With social media, however, we're served the equivalent of five plates of coleslaw all the time. People on their blogs post the same image repeatedly because they forgot they already posted it, or the same images appear over and over again on a Pinterest pinboard. On Facebook and Twitter, we expect the discrimination rule to be broken constantly: someone may tweet "10 days until the event!" followed up the next day with "9 days until the event" and the next day with "8 days until the event, sign up now!" While this repetition may be tolerable "conversation" on social networks, it doesn't fly as curation.

Academics who use curation-based research methods in their studies often find that some people discriminate more than others. In a study that reviews different methods of researching trends, they classify different discrimination styles as well. They call high discriminators "splitters" and low discriminators "lumpers." Lumpers minimize differences between items and create fewer but larger collections. These individuals tend toward detailing broader metathemes. Splitters, on the other hand, identify more differences between items and end up curating a larger number of smaller collections.[4]

Mutual Exclusivity

Katherine Accettura is a curator on Pinterest from Illinois. She has over 1.2 million Pinterest followers of her pin boards named "Fall + Winter Outfits," "I Can't Live Without," "Words of Encouragement," and "Food—Fresh and Healthy." For Accettura, it's important to discriminate among not only the content curated on a single board but also the content curated across boards. She thinks of her collection of collections as an act of curation as well. For example, she advises curators against "repeating" themselves by curating the same image onto multiple boards. As she says, "It is important to look at your pins as a whole entity. This will provide your followers with the most visually pleasing experience. Example: If you pin the same item to multiple boards in a row, they will show up as a duplicate pin to viewers on your Pinterest profile."[5] In summary, Accettura applies the discrimination rule across collections, not just inside them.

Holly Menard, a curator on Pinterest from Austin, Texas, with over 3 million followers, shares similar advice. For Menard, who curates collections such as "CHILDREN," "WATCH/READ," and, "INTERIOR," finding the collection with the exact right fit for a new piece of content is part of the challenge and fun of curation: "The most interesting thing to me about the process of pinning itself is the curating element. I enjoy the process of adding a pin to the board, which has the best aesthetic fit."[6] For Menard, the discrimination rule is intimately tied to defining that "fit."

With all the thought necessary to follow the discrimination rule and enforce the principle of mutual exclusivity, choosing to begin a new curated collection can be a big decision. It needs to be meaningfully distinct from preexisting collections and of enough depth to warrant committing the ongoing effort. Rowena Murillo, a Pinterest user with over 1.6 million followers, finds adding a new board to be nontrivial. She says that "My art and fauna board is one of my first boards. At first it was all animals, of every type, but then I had to open a 'cats and dogs' board for all the cuteness, because it did not fit with the mood of the board I really wanted. To me, it is about the wonder that is nature and the beauty of animals. I have been considering opening a new animal board . . . it's a tough decision though. I generally think on it for months before I open a new board, and then when I do, I wonder what took me so long."[7] Rather than one piece of content being enough to warrant a new board, Murillo waits (even months!) for a theme that's significantly distinct from her current collections; it's not a decision to take lightly.

While all well-curated collections adhere to the discrimination rule, collections can also have varying definitions of completion. In the next section we'll look at two of these types: infinite and finite.

Infinite versus Finite Collections

When you start curating a collection, it's worth considering what it will look like when it's finished. Depending on your answer, you'll discover if you've started either a finite collection or an infinite collection.

If you can imagine a time when your collection will be "done" or "perfect," then it's a finite collection. For example, a collection of the most interesting Coke bottles made before 2000 draws from a limited set of bottles and will eventually end. If you can't see an end in sight, then you may have embarked on an infinite collection. An infinite collection has potentially no upper limit because it is built according to a perspective. For example, a collection of the most interesting bottles, spanning all types including perfume bottles, drinking bottles, and bottles new and old, is open-ended and could continue to be curated continuously.[8]

Rowena Murillo, a teacher, writer, and artist from St. Petersburg, Florida, curates her interests across multiple pinboards when she feels inspired. For her over 1.6 million Pinterest followers, she curates into the topics she's most interested in at any moment (while letting others remain fallow too). In her words,

> I love all of my art boards (art and letters, art and portraits, art and illustration, etc. . . .). I love to look at them and be inspired. I love my geek and fangirl boards because that is where I put all my fantasy, sci fi, and comic book obsessions. I also love my cats and dogs board, because they just make me happy. I also love my Living the Life board. It's a sort of dream board in motion for me. . . . I find that I go through periods where I post more to one board, and less to others, as I take on different projects or emphasis in my daily life. I still love them, I just may not be actively engaged in them.[9]

For Murillo, most of her boards are infinite, and she migrates from board to board as her moods move her.

While collections can come to an end or go on forever, they can also move at different speeds. In the next section, we'll look at the principles behind fast and slow collections.

Fast versus Slow Collections

There are so many articles about cell phones that a curator could easily collect 20 of them a day. In contrast, Broadway musicals come out so infrequently that a curator may have the chance to collect one a month. With content moving at different speeds, it's important to consider if you're building a fast or slow collection (Figure 8.3). A fast collection requires a lot of attention

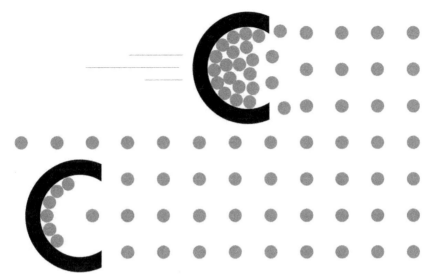

Figure 8.3

and offers continual updates for an audience. And just like cell phones, fast collections are also harder to keep up with. A slow collection requires less diligence but may not have the variety to support a daily audience. Who needs to visit your collection every day when it takes years to develop new Broadway shows? Depending on your curation goals and abilities, consider if you want a fast or slow collection.

Fast Content, Fast Trends

The fads and fashions that drive trends impact expensive and complex content much slower than simple, quickly developed content. The interior designer Katherine Bragg observes that the speed at which furniture design evolves is slower than some of her other projects, such as wall prints. She hypothesizes that this is because it's much more expensive and logistically difficult to experiment with couch manufacturing than with, say, a greeting card.

As an extreme example, it took over 1,000 years of construction and design for sports arenas and stadiums to evolve in major ways; comparing an open-air stadium from ancient Greece to modern stadiums is like comparing a hut to a skyscraper. But over a 10-year time frame, given that each stadium takes years and hundreds of millions of dollars to produce, the speed of stadium design trends is limited; there simply isn't enough reason or freedom to experiment with the design of something that's only commissioned and built a few times globally. Contrast that with recording a song, designing clothes, drawing a picture, or making a SpongeBob SquarePants meme that creators around the world can iterate quickly and cheaply. The rate of experimentation is much faster, as is the diversity of participants and ideas. As a result, if one graphic designer develops a compelling new font, other graphic designers can start using it immediately. If there is a new idiom in pop culture, such as something being "lit," there is little to no friction to a lyricist integrating it into her or his next song. But if a stadium designer makes a whole new design for an arena concession booth, at best it can be shared as a 3D model online or at an architecture show. For fast content, creators can participate in greater numbers and iterate more quickly. For curators, it means that the speed at which they need to keep up with and curate content can increase as well. After all, if you're a curator of stadiums, there are only a few to consider each year, and you can curate slowly. But if you're a curator of memes on Twitter, you'll be constantly underwater.

Curating is more than just keeping up with the speed of new content; it's also about recontextualizing and surfacing content from the past. In the next section, we'll consider the principle of looking forward and backward.

Looking Forward and Backward

The timeline is optional. To a curator, everything in the past and present is equally available and potentially relevant. And while curators can put a sensible chronology to good use, it's only one of many tools they may employ.

But for practical reasons, it's often sensible to specialize in either the past of the present. For example, an art curator at the Metropolitan Museum of Art is likely a historical expert skilled at understanding objects in the past, whereas an art curator at the Modern of Modern Art, while most likely also trained in art history, specializes in understanding the now and determining what's next. And while both of these curators would probably be better at each other's jobs than you or me, even they can't substitute for each other's years of expertise. For your collections, consider if you want to focus on the past, the future, or even both.

Arrangement

Without a layout you might as well throw a pile of pictures and articles in the air, because that's what your magazine will look like. Without placement you might as drop paintings around a room, because that's what your gallery will look like. And without a speaker order you might as well have Malcolm Gladwell speak at 3:00 a.m. in the parking garage, because your event will be just as messed up. A curator meticulously arranges content to communicate its meaning to an audience. Arrangement is a powerful nonverbal technique for establishing relationships, and there are four primary methods: sequence, clustering, grouping, and composition (Figure 8.4).

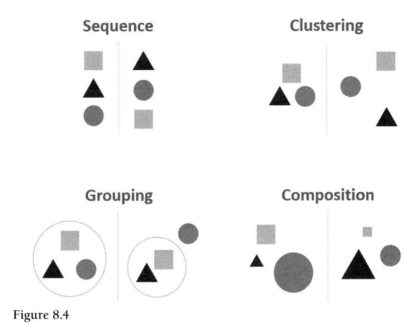

Figure 8.4

Sequence

The sequence is the order of the content's presentation. It may be as significant as the television network ABC deciding the hour to present the "Best Picture" award at the Oscars or as simple as switching the third and fourth songs in a party playlist. Regarding playlist order, two researchers at McGill University and the University of Victoria asked whether sequence order matters to the playlists developed by professional DJs. Unsurprisingly, when they asked DJs directly, they said "absolutely." Their quantitative measurements agreed with the DJ's opinions as well. As it turns out, DJs match the timbre (otherwise known as the sonic characteristics, or why a song sounds the way it does) much more closely between tracks than would otherwise happen at random (specifically, the researchers compared the timbre of the tracks in the order the DJs created versus a bunch of random orderings of the same songs).[10] So, while there are countless subjective reasons for why DJs sequence the way that they do, it's still possible to tease out some measurable patterns that demonstrate that order matters.

Clustering

Clustering implies association or disassociation between content based on the space between the content. For example, the Metropolitan Museum of Art may put paintings close together to suggest a connection while putting others at equal distances to suggest independence. At a music festival, certain bands may perform more or less close to each other based on their prominence. In a grocery store, the wine may be grouped with the beers because they're spirits, or they may be put in an entirely different area decorated with faux barrels and grapevines because they're artisanal. Clustering implies that items are part of a set.

Grouping

Grouping strengthens or diminishes associations by explicitly drawing "lines" between content in the same collection. For example, a single show at a gallery may span multiple rooms, with each room grouping the art, intentionally or not, into subsets of associations. Nightclubs employ grouping as well when they have two floors with different ambiences on each one.

Composition

The composition of a collection emphasizes or minimizes content with differences in size and appearance. For example, the prominence of a photograph increases if it's a wall-size print, and a painting more easily catches the eye when it's spot-lit. At a music festival, the main stage may be louder than the side stages and physically bigger as well. By altering the composition of a collection, a curator can guide our attention and draw emphasis.

Arranging within Constraints

Arrangement occurs within constraints of time and space. For material objects the constraints are physical, whereas for digital objects the constraint of time is typically more relevant (e.g., we can only program three hours of content before people leave, so how do we arrange what we have?). Interior designers are often constrained by the physical shape of a room. A merchandise manager of an app-based commerce website is often constrained by the limitations of the app design and the number of items that a smartphone screen can easily view. While you can imagine an infinite digital storefront (and even code it up), the practical reality is that people remain constrained by the size of their phone's screen, their laptop's monitor, or their own field of view in a virtual reality headset.

For the interior designer Katherine Bragg, the physical space directly impacts the layout of her furniture. In practice, she usually starts by drawing the physical space and figuring out how egress works (i.e., how people can come and go); moving through the space without disrupting its function is key. For example, you need to be able to arrange the couch, chairs, and coffee table in the salon so that people can easily chat but also make their way to the kitchen for hors d'oeuvres. Clustering and grouping principles become important the more functions one looks to include in a space—for example, doubling a living room as a working space or including a play area for kids in the living room as well. The more things people want to do in a space, the more challenging the clustering and grouping arrangement becomes. Bragg utilizes the concept of establishing zones within a space so that while the zones feel separate, the space actually remains whole. This enables a house to have a unified feel, but while you're actively doing a function (such as work), you can also feel separated without everyone being on top of each other all the time.

The arrangement of items takes on a particularly interesting dimension when you're done arranging and ready to share the final collection. In the next section, we'll look at how two primary ways of sharing collections impacts their reception.

Top-Down versus Bottom-Up Sharing

Let's say that you've redecorated your living room. It has an ivory-colored couch from Crate and Barrel, a decorative rhinoceros head hanging on the wall from Anthropologie, and Grandma's Persian rug. If you were to take a picture of your living room and post it on Instagram, you would be sharing your collection from the top down. Sharing from the top down means that you first present to people the completed collection (the photo of everything together) without necessarily the ability to follow up or investigate specific pieces. The strengths of this approach include preserving the curator's specific vision behind the arrangement of the objects in a particular space. There are several weaknesses, however; the first is that the audience can't easily learn about and follow up with the specific objects (e.g., where is the link to the rhino head? I like the Persian rug, but where can I get it or a similar one?). The second is that the curator can't easily curate another living room anytime soon (after all, the photo is of your own living room. What are you going to do, scrap everything and start over because you have a new idea?). Most platforms that focus on the editorial method of organizing subjectivity (such as Facebook, Twitter, Instagram, etc.) require sharing from the top down; you're either going to post that picture of your living room or not.

The alternative is sharing from the bottom up, which preserves the details of the individual pieces that were curated into the collection. The trade-off is that the arrangement is tied to the particular design of the digital platform, not the physical world. An example would be sharing your living room via a Pinterest board; you could pin the images of the couch and rhino head from their retailers' websites and either upload a picture of your grandma's rug or find a picture of a similar one; your audience could then follow up on the details of the specific pieces with the option to buy. This also means that you can curate lots of living rooms, assembling the pieces as you go within different collections. The weakness is that the arrangement remains a bit abstract; your audience, while looking at the set of images in a collage, needs to use some imagination as to how they'd fit together in a real room.

If you're not one to make compromises, it's also possible to share a curated collection from both the top down and the bottom up simultaneously. An example is a curated model living room in a furniture store. This model living room is fully curated from the top down with a sofa, a loveseat, an entertainment center, end tables, and coffee tables along with coffee-table books and floral bouquets arranged in a design for the space. It's curated from the bottom up too because you can investigate each piece one by one, following up on the price and manufacturer individually. The digital equivalent is Houzz.com, where (mostly) designers share images of projects they've completed and individual items in the photos of real homes are tagged, linking to an opportunity to purchase.

Sometimes curating from the top down and the bottom up are almost the same thing, as is the case for music playlists; whether you're looking at it from the top (a 60-minute mix) or the bottom (20 3-minute songs) it's still a list of songs; almost every playlist on Spotify accomplishes this. An exception to this would be a DJ's set of music where individual songs are played together in a single recording. With the songs unlisted and modified with tempo matching, fades, and elements of remixing, not only do you not know the specific songs, but even if you did, you couldn't go and retrieve them the same way because they only exist in that form in that recording.

With these new techniques you may feel like you're ready to jump in and start curating. But beware! There are several curation traps that undermine the value of curation entirely.

Curation Traps

Curation is an active, creative process that requires thoughtful attention; there are no shortcuts or quick fixes. People who try to short-circuit the process end up accumulating, aggregating, or acquiring content—and fall flat on their faces (Table 8.1).

Table 8.1 Curation requires classification, evaluation, and reframing

	Curating	Acquiring	Aggregating	Accumulating
Classify	✓	✓	✓	
Evaluate	✓	✓		
Reframe	✓			

Accumulation

Accumulation is the mindless, indiscriminate pursuit of more. Platforms such as YouTube, Imgur, and eBay accumulate content because they allow anyone to contribute whatever they want. The Internet itself accumulates content. The mind-set "let's accept everything and figure out if it's any good later" is accumulation mentality.

A lot of the Internet started with the accumulation mentality, because the first thing most engineers built were tools. For example, YouTube was first and foremost a tool to publish videos to the web; it was made first for video makers, not video watchers exactly. For example, the video-watching experience could be pretty terrible, but watchers would still suffer through it and marvel at the novelty. But if uploading the videos doesn't work, then there will be few to zero video makers and consequently few to zero watchers.

The same is true for eBay. The most important thing for the company to accomplish first was enabling sellers to sell and allowing auctions to accumulate on the platform. It's only with auctions in place that bidders can bid and make a transaction. If the fundamental ability to accumulate content isn't available, then most of these original businesses couldn't grow in the first place; they first need sellers auctioning and video makers streaming to attract bidders and watchers.

Aggregating

Aggregation is the indiscriminate but categorized pursuit of more. It's like the "Science & Technology" category on YouTube or eBay's lists of "mobile phones." The content is classified, and that's it.

For many Internet companies, aggregating becomes available after successfully mastering accumulation. It often comes second, because it's required to first master the tooling necessary to accept, store, and retrieve content (accumulate). After all, if you don't have content, you can't categorize it. It would be like a shoe marketplace start-up worrying about the finer distinctions in sneaker types before having any sneakers to sell.

Because aggregation is objective object categorization (e.g., it's a sneaker or a sandal), computers are often used to aggregate content automatically. Web companies that did this were even called "aggregators." For example, news aggregators might collect all the articles from the Associated Press, the *New York Times,* and the *Boston Globe* (among many more) and make them available in one place.

Acquiring

To acquire content is to collect as much content as possible that meets a set standard of quality, organizing subjectivity like an editor. For example, the Apple App Store requires that a new app meet a set of rules before it's accepted into the store. But as long as an app meets Apple's singular standard, the company will accept it. Same with Airbnb; as long as a submitted room meets a standard of quality, the company will accept it onto the platform.

Curation

Curated content is classified, evaluated, and reframed. Reframing occurs by developing a theme. Without a theme, the collection lacks the necessary subjective and aesthetic qualities. Without reframing, we're back to building messy warehouses of content, just like most websites on the early Internet. The Apple App Store is a good example of evolving from first acquiring to then curating. Today, the company have teams of curators classifying, evaluating, and reframing content according to themes that they think are interesting to help people navigate the millions of available apps.

Hoarding Disorder Addiction

In 2013, psychologists included the psychological condition of compulsive hoarding disorder addiction for the first time in the fifth edition of the *Diagnostic and Statistical Manual of Mental Disorders*. It's a condition whereby, for example, someone will fill her or his home floor to ceiling with newspapers and magazines and refuse to throw them away because they are "important." In 2014 a woman even died from it, as the sheer weight of the clutter caused the first floor of her home to collapse.[11] When we see people accumulate, aggregate, and acquire content in their homes like hoarders, we recognize that they may need help. If you wouldn't accumulate content like that in your home, then don't do it online either.

When one successfully avoids these traps and starts curating properly, there are many different styles of curation available. In the next chapter, we'll look at one way of exploring these curation styles. Which style describes you?

CHAPTER NINE

Curation Practices

The Six Curation Styles

What's your curation style?

Like jazz musicians, curators each have their own unique style. But like jazz music, there are stylistic "schools" of which all curators are a part. By identifying the way you mix popular and niche content, you can identify your own curation style—and even adopt a new one. And while no curation style is better than another, specific styles are more effective at accomplishing specific goals.

The long-tail diagram helps us visualize curation style (Figure 9.1). The head of the diagram displays mainstream content (such as *Harry Potter*), and the tail displays increasingly niche and unpopular content (such as your aunt's self-published memoir). The long-tail diagram demonstrates the reality that some content is really popular and that most everything else isn't.

Editor

The editor creates collections that appeal to mainstream audiences by curating popular content together. For example, an editor may make the collection "The Must-See Movies of Summer" and fill it with blockbuster action movies and romantic comedies. If you make content and an editor curates your work, the editor may confer mainstream status to your book, movie, or product that might be as of yet unknown.

Enthusiast

The enthusiast curates mainstream content to please niche audiences. For example, an enthusiast may make the collection "The Best Danny Elfman Film Scores" and fill it with soundtracks from *Men in Black, Spider-Man,* and

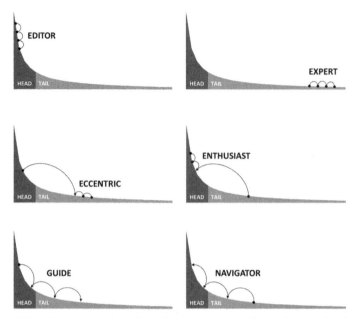

Figure 9.1 Curation styles described in terms of the long-tail of popular content.

Good Will Hunting. If an enthusiast curates your content, he or she can fire up a hard-core fan base, such as putting the soundtrack to *Spider-Man IV* into the hands of Danny Elfman fans before the film is out. The essence of the enthusiast is that he or she takes something more obscure (such as sound-tracks) and relates it to something popular (such as hit movies).

Eccentric

The eccentric curates collections seemingly directed at mainstream audiences but in fact fills the collections with idiosyncratic, niche content (eccentrics can seem a little off). For example, an eccentric may make the collection "Best Films of the Year" and then fill it exclusively with niche documentaries, because to the eccentric that documentary on yarn really was life changing. When your content is curated by an eccentric, this increases the chances that unforeseen niche audiences will pick up on your work.

Expert

The expert explicitly curates niche content for niche audiences. It's like making the collection "Best Documentaries on Typography" and actually filling it with documentaries about typography. Or like professors compiling articles into literature reviews. Curation by an expert connects your content with niche and likely rabid audiences.

Guide

The guide curates for a mainstream audience but fills collections with both mainstream and niche content. For example, a guide may create the collection "The Must-See Movies of Summer," fill it with blockbusters, and sneak in a few highly recommended independent films poised to be sleeper hits. Guides are skilled at introducing mainstream audiences to niche titles.

Navigator

The navigator creates collections directed at a niche audience and, like the guide, fills them with both niche and mainstream content. Where navigators differ is that they make the collection seem niche, such as "Best Documentaries on Weather." Because of their attention to niches, they're especially skilled at creating new ways of appreciating popular content. For example, a science professor who relates a study on carbon dioxide to the film *An Inconvenient Truth* curates like a navigator by convincingly connecting a niche study to a mainstream film.

Reflecting on your natural curation style and perhaps looking to develop others based on your goals is a great practice as an independent curator. However, when curating with others, this level of awareness becomes essential. In the next section, we'll look at how collaborative curation can bring you to new heights and how to avoid it bringing new lows.

Collaborative Curation

Collaborative curation can create heavenly results; it can also be a nightmare. Before starting any collaborative curation project, it's a good idea to address the following topics with your team.

Acknowledge That Good and Bad Taste Exists for a Team

Some people feel like it's politically incorrect to talk about good and bad taste; there can be a fear that good taste breeds intolerance. After all, if your taste is good, doesn't that mean other people's taste is bad? To maintain an atmosphere of inclusivity and tolerance, it's tempting to deny the notion of good taste and assert that all tastes are equal.

When you're collaborating, however, denying the notion of good taste doesn't work. In fact, asserting that all tastes are equal accomplishes the exact opposite and breeds an atmosphere of exclusivity and intolerance. How does this happen?

Let's say you're a curator of sculpture at the J. Paul Getty Museum and one of your colleagues wants to make an expensive acquisition that you and everyone else oppose on artistic merit. Ironically, if you can't debate the merits of good and bad art because all tastes are equal, there's no room to discuss, learn, and compromise. Without the ability to argue against bad acquisitions, everyone buys whatever they want, for any reason they want, for any price they want, like tyrants in their own fiefdoms. Ironically, in an attempt to be inclusive, denying good and bad taste encourages intolerance and makes teamwork impossible.

Alternatively, teams should focus on articulating standards of quality, principled perspectives and engaging with each other to meet those standards and uphold those principles. To deny that standards exist is to guarantee missing them.

Curate from the Top Down

Another strategy for facilitating collaborative curation is to align the curation efforts of your team by curating from the top down, which requires identifying a theme before making selections. This also establishes a reference point from which to argue for or against selections. Without this common ground, it's impossible to define a perspective and make decisions. Similarly, try avoiding bottom-up curation entirely. Curating from the bottom up is better suited to solo projects where there's latitude to grab whatever piques an individual's personal interest.

Explicitly Choose Either a Finite or Infinite Collection

Teams need milestones to gauge their progress, and these milestones will look different whether they're building a finite or infinite collection. For a finite collection, you may want to establish checkpoints with due dates. For an infinite collection, you may want to establish quotas. By choosing a finite or infinite collection, you can clearly define expectations and measure results.

Choose Curation Styles That Meet Your Goals

Do you need to appeal to as broad an audience as possible? Then make sure your team knows to curate like an editor. Do you want to promote a new product? Then direct your team to curate like a guide. If people know beforehand the best curation styles to adopt, they're more likely to meet their goal.

Similarly, if one person curates like an editor and the person's partner curates like an expert, they will almost inevitably butt heads and make a disjointed, hodgepodge collection. To grow curation assets in quality, not just quantity, try to coordinate the curation styles of your team.

Delegate Responsibilities

Surveying the landscape for new content is time-consuming, and making sense of old content can require a lot of expertise. Try delegating the responsibility of looking forward or backward based on people's skill sets and passions.

If you have a group of curators, learning the practice of collaborative curation can really help. But what if you're a maker or seller who wants to appeal to curators and get curated in the first place? In the next section, we'll look at how anyone can increase their chances of getting picked up by a curator.

Get Curated

So, you've got a new product and you want to get curated. To jump-start the curation process, there are several things that will increase your chances.

Reframe It

To notice your content, a curator needs to see how it fits with her or his interests—and may need some help. To help people see your product according to their own interests, reframe it. Create a context that emphasizes a value, practice, or attribute that typically goes unnoticed or may not exist yet. For example, one way to reframe your content is to develop and emphasize its aesthetics.[1] If you sell flatware, start selling beautiful flatware. If you make air-conditioning units, design a faceplate that's stylish instead of a gray, boxy eyesore: reveal the beauty in your product.[2]

Another approach is to release an aesthetically perfect version of your product. This could be as simple as high-resolution, top-notch photography. If the photo looks good, you're on your way to making the product look good.[3] It could also mean making an ornate version of your product. For example, when people hear about diamond-covered iPhone cases or bras, this infers that the specific brand of bra or case may be valuable in general (why else would it be covered in diamonds?). Reframing your content makes people think about it a different way.

Tell Your Story

Telling your product's story helps people understand and feel something for it.[4] Part of the marketing genius behind GoPro cameras is that the product itself is a storytelling device. All GoPro needs to do to tell stories is to show videos captured by its cameras. These videos provide potential curators with context to latch onto, such as "this is the definitive sports-action camera!" While not everyone sells cameras, every product has or can have its own story. For example, is there nostalgia around your product? Does it relate to an audience's shared history in any way? Is there notoriety around your product? Try answering these questions as a way to practice telling your story.

Present Variety

Products mean different things to different people; this is a good reason to present your product in different ways. By creating imagery of the same content in different contexts, you can increase the subjective hooks with which curators may resonate. For example, imagine a Patagonia jacket worn by a mountain climber on the summit of K2. Now, imagine the same jacket worn on the observation deck of the Empire State Building. In the first case, mountaineers may see the appeal. In the second case, urban adventurers may resonate with it. Another approach is to remove people from the photos altogether and allow curators to recontextualize the product according to their own perspective. There's data to support this approach too; by removing people from photos (and just showing the product itself), repinning on Pinterest increases 23 percent. When curators are most interested in the product itself, then a person is more of a distraction.[5]

Visual diversity also means presenting a neutral version of your product on a white or black background. This lack of context allows it to more easily assimilate into other settings.[6] The data shows that if the background represents too much of the photo, however, repins on Pinterest can decrease by up to half. The threshold is at about 40 percent. So, if you're taking a photo of a necklace, just make sure it represents 60 percent or more of the entire photographed area.[7]

Consider Modularity

Some products are by design meant to be mixed, matched, and curated. Take jeans, for example; they go with everything. You can wear shoes that are brown, black, or any other color. They're worn at picnics, by Silicon Valley CEOs, and by cowboys. While any particular pair of jeans may not be noticeable or unique, their modularity leads to high curatability. To the degree that your product is modular and easily repurposed, it will lend itself to curation.

Next, we'll look at the nature of digital collections themselves and how curation online has changed how customers fundamentally interact with and discover content. With this information, you'll learn how to best insert your content into this new digitally curated world.

CHAPTER TEN

The Collection

Everything Is Content

Things aren't things anymore: online, everything is content. Whether you're browsing landscapes on Instagram or used cars on eBay, the layout is almost always the same: a picture with some text. If it was stilettos, bulldozers, tickets to Fiji, or organic peanut butter, you'd still see a picture with some text. Online everything becomes content, and whether you want to be or not, everyone becomes a publisher.

You Are Your Media

Analysts expect one out of four malls in the United States to be out of business by 2022.[1] And while fewer stores translates into fewer in-store sales, it also marks the decline of stores as a destination to discover products. As the *Wall Street Journal* observes of the trend, "shoppers don't seem to be using physical stores to browse as much, either. Instead, they seem to be figuring out what they want online then making targeted trips."[2]

For example, a plush Mickey Mouse doll can "be itself" in a physical store; people can hold the doll and get a feel for it. The floor merchandiser can arrange the dolls at a child's eye level in poses with Mickey's friends Donald Duck and Minnie Mouse. Children can swing Mickey around and imagine themselves on an adventure with them—and then ask mom and dad to buy it.

Online, the same Mickey doll is a picture with a description, and a child's deciding moment happens between a swipe and a tap on a phone. The Mickey doll can't just be plush and inviting anymore; it has to be digital and photogenic. If products were like actors, it's as if roles are being given out based on headshots instead of auditions. With e-commerce, products can't just be products anymore; they're media.

In much the same way that products are now media, collections are now media as well. Next, we'll look at how digitization effects the collection itself.

Properties of a Collection

Environment

In addition to things not able to be "themselves" anymore, collections are also not able to be "somewhere." In a physical store, interior designers can transform store windows into safaris with binocular-using, vest-bearing mannequins; direct spotlights toward sparkling bottles of eyeliner; and design entire "living rooms" around an 80-inch TV so that when you first step inside, it already feels like that TV belongs in your home. Catalog designers have even more environmental control as they photograph Shawn White in a half-pipe riding his Burton snowboard, young women in overgrown English gardens modeling Anthropologie, or children catching the school bus wearing their L. L. Bean backpacks. Most websites, however, have backgrounds of white or taupe and show a few product photographs with supporting text. If traditional curators and designers could present their online collections as they do offline, the Internet would overnight become a more beautiful (and profitable) environment.

In 2007, the *Washington Post* ran an environment-based social experiment in collaboration with Joshua Bell, the world-famous Grammy Award–winning violinist.[3] They wanted to know if changing the environment in which Bell performs alters people's appreciation of his music. In the experiment, Bell wore a baseball cap and played violin for tips in a Washington, D.C., metro station. With one of the world's most talented violinists playing some of the most celebrated classical music on one of the best violins in the world, how much do you think he made in tips? How many people do you think stopped to listen? Over a 43-minute performance, 7 people stopped to listen for at least one minute out of a total of 1,070 people who hurried by without noticing (less than 1 percent stopped). Twenty-seven people tipped, giving a total of $32. In contrast, three days prior Bell played at a sold-out Boston Symphony Hall, where the average ticket price was around $100.

Why is it that Bell's performance in a symphony hall is worth hundreds of thousands of dollars, whereas his performance in the subway is worth $32? Why does one environment warrant the undivided attention of hundreds, whereas the other goes almost completely unacknowledged? Part of it has to do with people's state of mind while in the subway. For example, Bell wasn't even sure if people wanted him to be there: "When you play for ticket-holders . . . you are already validated. I have no sense that I need to be accepted. I'm already accepted. Here, there was this thought: *What if they don't like me? What if they resent my presence.*"[4] Outside of the familiar performance hall context, Bell questioned if people even wanted to hear his music. As the article's author observed of Bell, "he was, in short, art without a frame."

Another reason could be that the setting was so inhospitable that even if passersby did recognize it as great, they wouldn't have the time to stop for it. For example, I sometimes acknowledge the Golden Gate Bridge's greatness when I see it, but this doesn't mean that I stop what I'm doing, stare at it's grandeur, and sigh in marvel of modern engineering as I rush to work. It could be that many people recognized Bell's performance as great, and of those only seven had the time to stop and smell the proverbial roses.

But more likely, many people probably didn't recognize it as great at all. A man in a baseball cap playing music in a subway station looks too much like every other street performer, regardless of the quality of the music. It would be like laying Vincent Van Gogh's *Starry Night* among items in a garage sale. Is it a kitchy print? the real thing? cliché or priceless? There's no way to tell.

I spent some time in the music industry in Nashville, and there was a saying that "people like to hear what they like to see." The saying captured the idea that crafting and marketing an artist's image (especially through music videos) is just as important as, perhaps even more important than, the music itself. What industry veterans found is that if the image of the artist is right, they could still sell a bunch of records despite the music quality not being what they'd think is necessary to move that much product on its own. And the inverse is true too; a great musician with a forgettable image may never break through. Like Bell playing violin in the subway, the environment in which people "see" the music heavily impacts their appreciation of hearing it.

Title and Description

Advertisers call a description copy and use it to persuade. Artists consider titles a part of their art. In both cases, before anyone has the chance to see a collection, they will likely read the title and description of it. Like a movie trailer, it may be the primary basis with which people decide if they want to view a collection at all. And like the cover of a magazine, it's one of the few ways to explicitly communicate a collection's focus and purpose.

For example, which natural history exhibit would you rather see, *Mesozoic Fauna* or *Real-Life Monsters*? Both feature the same bones of a T rex, but the latter is almost guaranteed 10 times as many visitors. A compelling title and description is critical to success.

In addition to the environment, title, and description of a collection, there are other ingredients that can make it of higher quality. Next, we'll look at many of the basic attributes of high-quality collections.

Attributes of High-Quality Collections

As you curate more and more, you'll quickly find that if unchecked, collections can become unwieldy. These next several techniques will help you retain the quality of your collection of collections.

Alignment

A store hangs a sign that says "Pizza," but inside it's a hardware store. This store needs better alignment between its title and its content. Curated collections are the same. They don't have to have literal descriptions such as "cars," but they can't be deceptive either. For example, a collection called "Stylish Sports Cars" filled with carpet samples lacks alignment. It may very well be a great collection of carpet samples, but without a useful title, it loses value.

Mutual Exclusivity

If a publication recycles articles from month to month, there's less of a reason to read it. The same is true for curation. If the same content repeats across collections, there's less of a reason to keep browsing. So, if you want to curate "Stylish Sports Cars," "Top European Roadsters," and "My Favorite Cars," make sure they are truly mutually exclusive.

Attribution

Imagine a film that didn't tell you the names of the actors in the credits. What if you really liked an actor's performance and wanted to learn more about that person? You'd be hung out to dry.

Good curators attribute content because they expect deeper engagement and want to help others learn about the content as well. This also signals expertise and professionalism by demonstrating knowledge of a content's origin. It's like a person who doesn't just know an actor's name but can name the other movies the actor has been in too: it's obvious that the person knows what he or she is they're talking about.

Attribution has the added benefit of sanitizing content for resharing. Without it, a curator exposes himself and resharers to unintended infringement accusations. Good curators don't create liabilities for themselves or their audiences, and many would rather not curate at all than disrespect the content they enjoy and its creators.

Attribution leads us to another important topic: intellectual property. As it turns out, content isn't the only thing covered by Internet protocol protections; the curated collection is protected as well.

Intellectual Property

U.S. copyright law protects curated collections as intellectual property. A collection is considered copyrightable "compilation" if "the materials are selected, coordinated, or arranged in such a way that the resulting work as a whole constitutes a new work."[5] This includes compilations such as your favorite restaurants in New York City, a list of the best short stories of 2011, a playlist of the top hits in 2004, a book of the greatest news photography, an online photo gallery, an academic journal, a newspaper of articles by different journalists, or a print catalog.

The record label Ministry of Sound tested this copyright in 2013 by suing Spotify in British courts, claiming that Spotify infringed on the ministry's compilations.[6] For over 20 years the Ministry of Sound has made dance music compilations, with more than 50 million albums sold. On Spotify, users were remaking these compilations for anyone to stream freely. By March 2014 the Ministry of Sound settled with Spotify, which agreed to remove playlists from its search engine and prevent users from following the playlists made by others. So, while most curators embrace sharing, it's worth considering that if you choose to turn curated works into products, they are protected and defendable.

So far in Part III, we've looked at curation concepts, principles, and practices and, in this section, the collection itself. The next section looks at the motivation and skills you can tap into right now to start curating at your best.

CHAPTER ELEVEN

Start Curating

Find Your Motivation

> Work and play are words used to describe the same thing under differing conditions.
>
> Mark Twain

If you haven't started curating by now, then get excited. About anything. If you don't care about what you're curating, other people won't either. The best curators have strong passions and leverage many personal motivations. Which will you tap into?

Fun

Indulging in what you enjoy can feel like play. Curating for fun allows people to fantasize about possible futures or impossible ones. It expresses parts of ourselves—like the desire to join the circus—that we may not otherwise get to explore and indulge in.[1] But in the process of finding trapeze camps for adults, juggling schools, and an uncertified lion-taming class in Thailand or perhaps searching for circus posters, circus tents, and popcorn machines, you can feel the fun of indulging the circus fantasy.

Creativity

Curation is a creative act; the collection is something you build. For people who don't know how to draw or write poetry or songs but still want to be creative, curation is a widely accessible outlet for self-expression.[2] And if you're questioning the creative merits of curating content, don't tell that to anyone who's slaved over the perfect mixtape, obsessed over the perfect date-night outfit, or researched the best portfolio of stocks. Selecting content that goes well together is a typewriter for those who can't write, a paintbrush for those who can't paint, and a pair of ballet slippers for those who can't dance.

Mastery

Curating an incredible collection of Amish furniture won't get you a PhD, but you may become an authority nonetheless. Curation offers a unique opportunity to develop distinction and mastery around any interest.[3] Just look at the wide variety of Pinterest users, playlist makers on Spotify, bloggers, and Instagrammers who have amassed a following due to sharing their subjective mastery. Accruing authority is more available today than ever before as an endless variety of subjective perspectives find their audiences.

Preservation

Is there something you care about that you feel is being lost to the sands of time? For many people, it can feel like we're missing what's important for what's new. Curation as a preservation activity brings focus to content and ideas that you feel deserve lasting attention.[4] For example, is there music from the 1970s that you think could be appreciated today if it only had a champion who would stand up for it? Is there a way to preserve the art of coin collecting so that millennials have a chance to learn and experience the hobby despite the rise of digital currencies such as Bitcoin? If so, then preservation may be a motivation for you to start curating today.

Adventure

Exploring new content can feel like an adventure: given enough cunning, skill, and luck, you may discover your next great find.[5] For a curator on the hunt, nothing feels quite as good as the satisfaction of a new discovery. If you like the feeling of a treasure hunt, curation can provide it. For example, are you completely familiar with every pair of jeans at the mall? Do you get a thrill when you find a standout pair at the local consignment shop or a new line of jeans that is just released by your favorite brand? Than curating with a sense of adventure may appeal to you.

Curation Can Also Be Work

Curation can also be hard work. While it may be fun to pick out things you like, once you want to discover likable things on a schedule, you quickly realize that you need to spend quite a bit of time assessing things that you don't like. For Jennifer Moen from Indiana, who has over 90,000 followers on Pinterest, it started with the desire to learn how to cook and led to a work-like intensity for curating recipes. She says that "it all started with my interest in learning how to cook and my growing love for food. I explored food blogs like it was my job, and pinned recipe after recipe, and people must have been drawn to that."[6] So while it's important to tap into a variety of motivations, it's also worth keeping in mind that if curation is pursued with intensity, regularity, and expectations and timelines around output, it can be a lot of work too.

But it's not just about motivation; curation requires hard skills too. In the next section, we'll look at ways you can develop your curatorial skills as well.

Develop Your Skills

If you indulge your curatorial passions and start actively curating, the skills will naturally follow. To help you on your journey, there are four major curation skills to develop.

Content Expertise

Developing content expertise is like learning to taste wine: there are important differences and subtle nuances in every bottle, and there's no substitute for actually doing the tasting. As you explore and learn about your tastes, you'll learn to identify these differences for all kinds of content, whether it be antiques, electronics, or stuffed animals. For example, you'll know you've started developing content expertise when a parent asks you "Which stuffed animal is best for my toddler?" and the question comes across as overly simplistic (what do you mean by "best"? Are we judging based on materials, design, price, brand?). But nonetheless, you're still able to make a helpful recommendation while providing a menu of alternatives as well.

Breadth of Knowledge

Asking a toy store employee which stuffed animal is best is like asking prison inmates about their favorite board games: they'll probably go on at length about the merits of checkers, but in the end you just don't care because of their limited knowledge.

Interesting collections require a breadth of knowledge. While someone may be enthusiastic for a specific piece of content (e.g., "I love Disney's *Frozen*!"), specific pieces of content do not constitute a collection. Without a breadth of knowledge about *Frozen*'s predecessors and influences, it's almost impossible to curate a meaningful collection.

Taste Leadership

Taste leadership is the ability to identify what's next. There's no formula for it, yet it exists. People who have it typically know what has come before and are plugged into today's popular and up-and-coming creators. They're able to align their tastes with the masses and, like weather forecasting, predict where the wind will blow next. While you might not be able to get it right all of time (weather forecasters don't either), if you work at it, you can get it right more of the time. And like a good investor, while a large part of the job is saying "no," the real trick is learning when to say "yes" and double down.

Storytelling

Imagine the first floor of the Louvre with the paintings taken down, slotted into a steel box, and rolled into a closet. While that closet may contain one of the best art collections of all time, much fewer people will choose to visit it. The storage of art in a box reduces a world-class exhibition into an exercise in packing.

Good curators use storytelling techniques, such as developing an environment and crafting a narrative, to communicate their ideas. They care deeply about where a collection is displayed, such as inside a palace, and how it's displayed, from the picture frames to the spot lighting. It's through these elements of craft that a curator gives a collection life, takes us on a journey, and expands our horizons.

In Part III so far, we explored many of the nuts and bolts of curation. And despite curation being a subjective process, there are a lot of specific actions to consider! But the fundamental subjective immeasurability of what constitutes good and bad curation creates many complications. In the next chapter, we'll explore what it looks like to curate in a subjective world where there is no objective good or bad and equip you with the frameworks you need to not only avoid common problems but also think critically about your own curation strategy.

CHAPTER TWELVE

Curate in a World without Good or Bad Taste

While curators on collaborative projects should align on principles of good taste, their audiences have no such alignment. As a result, how does one curate well and make quality recommendations in a world without good or bad taste? What does it mean that "good" is relative to people and, as a result, is also a moving target? To explore this question, we'll dive into the relativity of taste itself and explore how its relative nature affects enjoyment and pleasure. While it might feel unsettling to retire the notion of content being objectively good or bad for everyone, it in fact liberates us from the deceit that it's possible to curate the "perfect" collection for everyone. It's by embracing relativity that we can appreciate that everyone comes from somewhere and that their ways of experiencing enjoyment is contextual. So, let's jump into the deep end and explore the first of many counterintuitive truths that taste relativity presents. To start, there are in fact no objectively good or bad smells.

There Are No Good or Bad Smells

The relativity of good and bad begins at the most fundamental, seemingly inalterable level: our senses. To start, consider the sense of smell on garbage day. When I used to walk around in New York City during the summer, once a week the streets would become lined with leaking walls of curbed garbage bags. Over time out of fear of waves of rotting food and roasting baby diapers hitting my nostrils, I stopped breathing through my nose (even on nongarbage days). Yet when I revolt at the smell of rotten milk searing on the sidewalk, my brain's interpretation that sulfides smell bad is actually relative to my personal experience and is not objectively bad. How so? Well, in countries where private plumbing isn't widely available, people report that the pervasive smell of sewage isn't offensive.[1] Essentially, since I'm not exposed to it very much and am exposed only in negative contexts, it remains offensive to me. As another example, in areas of the world where the dead are burned as part of the burial ceremony, the scent of burning flesh isn't reported as a bad smell. Ostensibly, if I lived in a culture where burning flesh was common, I wouldn't think of it as a bad smell either.

Rachel Herz, a psychologist at Brown University, specializes in the study of smell and finds that "In smell there is one absolute truth: everything is relative." In her research, she find that "no odors are inherently repugnant; we learn our emotional responses to them through either experience or culture."[2] As an example from her own life, Herz learned to like the scent of skunk from her mother's influence. I relate to that personally, as skunks became more and more associated with my cool evening jogs through the woods. There are industrial examples too. For example, smell relativity has hampered the military's development of a general stink bomb. The military has gone through the effort of making terrible smells, and then inevitably there is some culture that shrugs it off. And the reverse is true as well; as Herz points out, it's hard to find smells loved everywhere (although vanilla comes pretty close).

Experience and culture can teach us to dislike smells too—even smells we previously liked. For example, I used to love pecan pie until it coincided with a dinner that gave me food poisoning. To this day, the smell of pecan pie (even typing these words) makes me queasy. Similarly, I used to really enjoy the smell of wood fires; years of camping and wood-burning stoves created deep, positive associations. Yet by the third day of heavy forest fire smoke from the northern California fires saturating San Francisco (destroying at least 8,400 homes),[3] I started to hate the smell. Somewhere between wearing a facemask, the headaches, and the sky glowing red like an apocalypse, a wood fire started to smell less like camping on cozy New England nights and more like lung cancer and tragedy.

This connection between lived experience and smell preference caught Herz's attention as well. To investigate, she performed a study that measures the mind and body connections in odor preference formation. In the study, she exposed two groups of students to an unfamiliar odor while they completed tasks on a computer for cash rewards. In one group the tasks were frustrating, and when asked how they liked the scent afterward, the students reported disliking it. Conversely, the second group had easy tasks and reported liking the scent afterward. As it turns out, the preference for the smell was heavily influenced by the preference for the overall experience; the smell itself had the potential to be either liked or disliked.

While it may be surprising that there are no universally good or bad smells and that the smells you like or dislike can even flip-flop, we're about to go down the relativity rabbit hole even further. We're going to look at a class of preferences that people like specifically because they dislike it.

Hurts So Good

Liking something because you've always liked it or learning to like something because of new positive associations makes sense. A lot of the time we may not even know why we like something; we just like what we like. But what about liking something because we dislike it? Masochism is the classic condition of taking pleasure in pain. And it's tempting to write it off as an abnormality affecting only a small percentage of the population.

While full-fledged masochism may be rare, its little brother, which researchers call benign masochism, is not. If you've ever expressed a sentiment such as "it hurts so good," then you're a benign masochist. Examples include burning your mouth with spicy foods, experiencing pain during a massage, loving to cry to sad movies or songs, being physically exhausted from a hard workout, liking bitter foods such as coffee or chocolate, enjoying scary experiences such as a horror house, or drinking in excess. Benign masochism is a common expression of a hedonic reversal: sources of pain that cause pleasure.[4] Central to the experience of hedonic reversals, however, is that there is really little to no risk of actual harm. This implies a certain distancing from a safe threat, such as roller coasters.[5] The thrill comes from your mind knowing that you're safe but your body feeling that it's not. If you really believed that you might fly off the tracks, it would be a genuine threat; terror would strike your mind and body, and you'd never do it again.

Some horrible experiences attract thousands of visitors just to be part of the hedonic reversal. For example, people show up en masse to the Chicago Botanic Garden for a chance to smell the corpse flower, which blooms up to 10 years apart and only for 8 to 12 hours. Everyone knows that it will smell like rotting death, yet they line up for blocks to experience it anyway. Studied by researchers from Yale University, the University of Pennsylvania, and West Chester University, they conceive of hedonic reversals as a form of competence demonstration, or the feeling of pleasure from overcoming a difficult situation. They observe that "This realization that the body has been fooled, and that there is no real danger, leads to pleasure derived from 'mind over body.' This can also be framed as a type of mastery."[6] From this perspective, hedonic reversals generate pleasure from pain because of the control of self and the situation involved.

Liking things you disliked, disliking things you liked, and then liking things because you dislike like them are just a few of the ways that good and bad are relative. Next, we'll look at yet another variable in the equation of taste relativity: preferences are relative to other people too.

Good Is Relative to People

If there is no objective good that's true for everyone, then what does it mean to say "I think cilantro tastes good"? As far as the brain is concerned, it means that for that person, it evaluates the senses involved and considers them positive. There is no celestial culinary judge presiding over a divine kitchen proclaiming some foods as tasty and others as gross. For people whose brains tell them that cilantro tastes bad, it really does taste bad—period. And while you don't have to enjoy country music, if Uncle Bob does, then that's objectively true for him; he really does like it. And if his preferences change toward organ music and country loses its appeal, then that's true too; Uncle Bob doesn't like country music anymore.

Thinking of things as good and bad extends beyond an individual and into groups as well. For example, if everyone in the country thinks that the national anthem is patriotic and that patriotism is good, then the national anthem will be considered good too. In fact, it becomes a social "fact" that the national anthem is good, and given the sheer number of people who like it, it may seem objectively good. For those born and raised in a country where the national anthem is considered good, it could seem as permanent as the sun rising. Alternatively, if patriotism becomes linked with something unpopular (such as cultural insensitivity), it can transform the national anthem into something not just disliked but also, if enough people dislike it, even objectively bad. For people who grow up learning that patriotism is exclusionary, this can become a "fact" to them, as seemingly permanent as the sun rising.

Whether it's with groups or individuals, preferences are inherently relative to people. To complicate matters further, preferences fall in and out of popularity for the same groups and individuals. For example, perhaps you love a song one week, but then a month later you don't listen to it anymore. Or a dress is a must-have one season and then old news the next. As the pioneering fantasy writer George Macdonald describes it in his book *What's Mine's Mine,* "They had a feeling, or a feeling had them, till another feeling came and took its place. When a feeling was there, they felt as if it would never go; when it was gone they felt it had never been; when it returned, they felt as if it had never gone."[7]

What drives preference changes within a person? For your own product, business, or content, get excited for the next section; you'll learn about fundamental psychological dynamics that explain why things fall in and out of popularity and gain insights into how you can work with these changes instead of against them.

CHAPTER THIRTEEN

Similarity and Difference

In the next few sections, we'll look at three theories that inform why things change in popularity: the Wundt curve, the horizon of expectation, and the zone of proximal development. These theories cut across several academic disciplines including psychology, cultural theory, and educational psychology, but across all of them is a common dynamic that affects preferences: similarity and difference. We'll start with the Wundt curve, grounding ourselves in a perspective from the field of psychology.

The Wundt Curve

Wilhelm Wundt was a 19th-century physician, philosopher, and professor and one of the fathers of psychology as a discipline (he founded the academic branch of experimental psychology itself).[1] The Wundt curve (Figure 13.1), which he proposed originally in 1874[2] (and was enhanced by Berlyne in 1971),[3] demonstrated in the laboratory that pleasure increases with novelty to a point, after which the experience gets too weird, people turn off, and it becomes unpleasurable. It's a type of Goldilocks theory whereby in the case of maximizing pleasure, something can't be too familiar or too novel; it needs to be "just right" to feel the best.

Take jazz music, for example. Let's say you decide to visit the jazz lounge Papa Bear, and the jazz quartet is playing a nursery room, childlike version of "Twinkle Twinkle Little Star." You hardly notice it at first, but when you do, you hope that they spice it up a bit—but it never happens. They play "Twinkle Twinkle Little Star" entirely straight, and you can never get those three minutes of your life back. In terms of the Wundt curve, you experienced too little novelty to feel pleasure and didn't receive a hedonic reward.

The next evening, you choose to visit a different jazz lounge called Mama Bear. Oddly enough, the jazz quartet there is also playing "Twinkle Twinkle

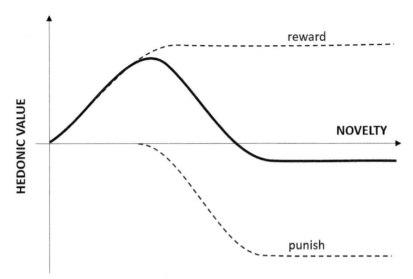

Figure 13.1 The Wundt Curve illustrates that pleasure increases with novelty up to a certain point.

Little Star" but this time in a completely different way. Tonight's version contains so much variation and dissonance that you could have sworn they forgot to tune their instruments or were perhaps just playing notes at random. Unable to ground yourself in the performance, you cut your night short after developing a pounding headache. On the Wundt curve, you experienced too much novelty to experience pleasure and as a result experienced displeasure (a hedonic punishment).

Before switching to country music bars and giving up on jazz completely, you give it one more shot and visit a jazz club called Baby Bear. The jazz group there is also, coincidentally enough, playing "Twinkle Twinkle Little Star" but this time decided to mix in the theme from "Let It Be" by the Beatles. The resulting tune combined both the familiarity of a dear childhood memory with the nostalgia of a classic smash hit. Engaged from the start, it puts you on the edge of your seat. Excited by what this group will play next, you know exactly where you'll go next: the tip jar. This time around on the Wundt curve, you experienced just enough novelty to receive pleasure (a hedonic reward) because there wasn't too much variation or too little.

The Wundt curve helps us understand that novelty—that's neither too much or too little but just right—is key to eliciting pleasure. For a curator or content creator looking to be well received, it's important to consider that creating something different is essential to engaging audiences but that too much difference may accomplish the opposite.

Yet, what's just right for one audience may be considered too much or too little for a lot of other people; it always comes down to the specific audience. After all, even though we didn't like the jazz fusion at the Mama Bear lounge, the club was still full of people. How can we better identify the line that divides too much from too little? How can we best recognize it so that we can produce content that rides that line without going too far in either direction? In the next section, we'll look at a theory called the horizon of expectation that will give us tools for identifying that line and delighting audiences.

Horizon of Expectation

> A literary work is not an object which stands by itself. . . . It is not a monument. . . . It is much more like an orchestration which strikes ever new chords among its readers . . . and makes it meaningful for the time.
>
> Hans Robert Jauss

While the Wundt curve communicates that some novelty is captivating while too much is off-putting, it doesn't go far enough. For example, how do we think about some things being too novel for me but not novel enough for you and the thousands of variations in between across millions of topics and interests? Or how do we think about the fact that sometimes the whole world seems to agree that something is amazing (e.g., Taylor Swift), yet some things that used to be normal are now passe (such as gendered bathrooms)? Jauss and his theory of the horizon of expectation gives us a framework to not just think about these phenomena but also act on them.

The horizon of expectation is part of Hans Robert Jauss's 1970s reception theory. Reception theory is a fancy term to describe the study of what audiences think of content when they experience it. Jauss proposes that each person contains a horizon of expectations that they bring to all the content and products they consume. Each person's horizon has a unique shape that's continually molded by every new experience. For example, the last book you read shaped the expectations you brought to this book, influences your interpretation of it, which in turn shapes the expectations you bring to the next book. Looking at it another way, imagine that you're reading for the first time a story about a prince saving a princess where they live happily ever after; it would be thrilling! However, if you've seen this trope 100 times across books and movies, reading it again would be at best predictable or at worst cliché and tired. This reaction would mean that the plot device now falls deep within the horizon of expectations (similar to if a story doesn't have enough novelty on the Wundt curve). However, if the story had been about a starfish's imperialist dream to colonize the land, it would be so far outside our horizon of expectations that we couldn't make heads or tails of it—even if starfish find it thrilling.

Now, let's say there's an experience just outside the horizon. For example, a story where a prince goes to save a princess but—twist!—the princess saves herself and the prince to boot. Jauss calls this distance outside the horizon the "aesthetic distance," and similar to the Goldilocks nature of the Wundt curve, a creative work can't be too close to the horizon of expectation or too far from it. There exists some maximal aesthetic distance that is both accessible yet provoking, familiar yet strange, known yet puzzling. And a single audience's reaction can be varied depending on the shape of their horizon, experiencing reactions such as "spontaneous success, rejection or shock, scattered approval, or gradual and later understanding."[4]

The horizon of expectation builds on the Wundt curve by describing the contours of what one thinks is novel across an entire range of interests, creating space for the contour to change shape over time. For example, experiencing the aesthetic distance of a princess saving a prince results in a horizon change that alters the contours of the reader's horizon. The novelty of the story changed the reader's expectations of what a story could be and as a result of traveling this "aesthetic distance" causes it to be less novel when it next comes along. Eventually, when you've read and watched it 100 times across books and movies, it becomes just as boring as the traditional narrative, and the desire to travel the aesthetic distance and experience a horizon change returns. The next interesting narrative may be of a princess who rules a kingdom on her own, whereas if you had tried to tell that story first, audiences may have rejected it as going too far (from their horizon of expectations).

Differently Shaped Horizons

Everyone has differently shaped horizons. This explains why some folks are really into things that others can't relate to. For example, I can't relate (at all) to the sport of dressage. Dressage is a form of horse training and exhibition where both the rider and the horse dress up and perform routines for an audience. The riders will wear tuxedos, for example, and the horses will have their hair braided and groomed like they're going to a ball. The routine looks a lot like choreography as the rider directs the horse through highly practiced and technical steps.

Dressage is so far outside of my horizon of expectations that, if you told me it were a *Saturday Night Live* skit, I'd believe you. But for people who follow dressage (it's an Olympic event, after all), it's thrilling to see the horse perform a difficult dance move. The shape of their horizon, formed by years of exposure to horses, positions each new advancement in technique within an accessible aesthetic distance, and they can appreciate it. Next year may be a different story once every horse starts doing the same move, but for now, their experience of the horizon shift is thrilling.

For me, however, the aesthetic distance is so far that my eyes glaze over. But that doesn't have to remain the case. There could exist a dressage appreciation class capable of reshaping my horizon such that I too jump for joy with each and every dance performance. This curriculum could ease me into the idea of horseback riding with a slate of westerns that first glorify the rider/horse bond. Next, I could try horseback riding and immediately realize that there's nothing simple about riding a 1,000-pound animal, even for a lap around the track. After a few lessons I could come to realize just how big the horseback riding learning curve really is, putting into perspective the magnitude of other's accomplishments and my own deficits. From my newly calibrated horizon, I may start feeling a rush of excitement while watching a rider on a horse performing intricate footwork; the aesthetic distance would be in reach. But until the shape of my horizon changes, I won't be in a position to care and will likely point and snicker at all the riders attending horse prom.

The Average Horizon

While everything people experience modifies their horizon of expectations, if lots of people experience the same thing, the shape of all of their horizons can shift in similar directions. For example, cultural moments that affect an entire society, such as 9/11, Hurricane Katrina, and the death of Michael Jackson affect millions of people in related ways, synchronizing their horizons to some degree (e.g., radio stations played Michael Jackson for two weeks straight after he died, educating everyone who may not have known about him that he's a big deal). Cultural moments can trigger horizons to shift in unison across a population, averaging the shape of millions of people's horizons at once. From this shared foundation, aesthetic distances can be traveled by the masses simultaneously, causing their already averaged horizon to shift in unison. One could imagine that after every cultural moment, world event, hit movie, song, or book, the mass culture becomes newly primed for another cultural moment. For example, the singing group Boyz II Men may have laid the groundwork for the boy band sound of the 1990s, from which the Backstreet Boys benefited. And it's possible that from the foundation of hundreds of millions of people loving the Backstreet Boys, 'N Sync was then able to stimulate another horizon shift with their smash hit "Bye Bye Bye." It may have been the right content to travel the next aesthetic distance for a preconditioned audience.

Some people are exceptionally good at recognizing population-wide horizons of expectation and can spot the next thing capable of traveling the aesthetic distance. I was able to experience a little of this firsthand while in Nashville, Tennessee, exploring what it would be like working in the music industry. While there, I heard a talk by the head of A&R (artists and repertoire) at a top 4 record label (A&R is the division of a record company responsible for scouting new talent and developing the current roster of acts). When hopeful bands send in their demo to a record company hoping to get discovered, it's someone in A&R who gets their package and listens to their demo (or, more often, doesn't listen to their demo). The story goes that the most successful member of this A&R executive team had a track record of discovering more hit artists than anyone else. Immediately I started imagining this superstar A&R employee as a master cool hunter, a sort of rockstar hit maker with his finger on the pulse of music and society. He must be someone who pushes the boundaries of what's cool and interesting in his own life, most likely drives a sports car, has an asymmetrical haircut, wears toe rings not because they're cool but because they're going to be cool, and discusses the finer points of Buddhism en route from teaching yoga to a weekend snowboarding group in Peru.

I was completely wrong.

The only exceptional thing about their top hit finder was that he was entirely unexceptional. He liked fast food and drove his nuclear family around in a minivan. He got haircuts from the local barber, watched NASCAR, preferred his sandwiches on Wonder Bread with plenty of mayonnaise, and couldn't touch his toes, let alone practice yoga. He was in average shape, of average height, entirely content to live an average life in Tennessee. And this A&R manager knew that it was precisely this averageness that made him great. His tastes weren't developed and out of touch as with a master critic, caught up in the subtle nuances that only a trained ear could detect. He had no formal music training and wasn't impressed by the "genius" artistry created by artists in the avante-garde. As a result, his ears remained calibrated with the average American who also eats fast food, loves football, and has a balance of $5,000 on her or his credit cards. You could say that this employee's horizon of expectations was in line with the average horizon. As a result, when he liked something, the record company had a pretty good guess that the aesthetic distance he was traveling wasn't very far—like most of America.

So, if audiences have horizons of expectation, it makes sense that content too far outside or inside would be considered unappealing or boring. But what about content that is within the aesthetic distance or just outside of it? What if you're not sure how far from someone's frontier your content lies, but you'd like to increase the chances that it's received and enjoyed by them? To answer that question, we'll move into the field of developmental psychology and tap into the study of how the brain learns and travels this distance in the first place.

Zone of Proximal Development

Google can bring you back a hundred thousand answers. A librarian can bring you back the right one.

Neil Gaiman

The zone of proximal development was conceived by the Soviet psychologist Lev Vygotsky (1896–1934) during the last 10 years of his life before dying at the age of 37 of tuberculosis. Vygostky is considered one of the most eminent psychologists of the 20th century and his concept of the zone of proximal development teaches us that we can't immediately understand everything on our own,[5] but with some assistance we can get there.

For example, sometimes you can immediately enjoy something, such as Disney World. There are experiences and content that are strategically designed to appeal across generations to both the young and the old, with themes and characters that are immediately relatable. Other times, people will experience something new and be like "hunh"? For example, art house films leave me completely stranded; I don't understand what's going on or why everyone around me is swooning intellectually. And then there are things in the middle (another form of Goldilocks theory) that, with a little help, you can enjoy and understand. The zone of proximal development represents these concepts and ideas in the middle. It's the realm of things that are outside your reach but no so far away that someone can't help you get there.

Vygotsky is a fixture in education literature because many of his theories of cognitive development are based on how children learn. But many of his theories apply to how the mind in general develops. For example, he describes how the mind has functions that are fully developed (such as our ability to appreciate Disney World) and functions that are in a fledgling state, such as how many people may feel about kombucha (fermented tea) or powdered peanut butter right now (it's dehydrated and goes great in smoothies apparently). In Vygotsky's words, "The zone of proximal development defines those functions that have not yet matured but are in the process of maturation, functions that will mature tomorrow but are currently in an embryonic state. These functions could be termed the 'buds' or 'flowers' of development rather than the 'fruits' of development. The actual developmental level characterizes mental development retrospectively, while the zone of proximal development characterizes mental development prospectively."[6] In other words, the zone of proximal development describes what you're able to understand next.

While the Wundt curve and the horizon of expectation look closely at how individuals and audiences react to and enjoy novel content, the zone of proximal development is much less passive; it illustrates that people can proactively intervene and change how others react to content. In fact, it shows that there are entire classes of content that someone can only appreciate with assistance. Far from just understanding how people interpret content, the zone of proximal development explains, for example, that curators are in a position to change the frontiers of their audiences' expectations, proactively guiding people toward experiences and interpretations they could not have arrived at in isolation. It's like being at a chocolate tasting, learning that a participant loves milk chocolate, and easing the participant into 50 percent dark chocolate first. While it would be a mistake to just hand the participant 85 percent dark chocolate ("too bitter!"), it's possible by the end of evening to ease her or him into ever darker pieces. The challenge of the curator in this case is to bridge this taste gap.

My friend Joseph Nagle, a designer at Google, helped me bridge a taste gap that I wouldn't have been able to do on my own. I had been asking him for design advice for the start-up I was working on at the time, especially around user experience and—the bane of many entrepreneur's existence—the logo design. The process of designing a logo threw me further into the field of typography than I ever thought I'd venture. But as a result, when Gary Hustwit's film *Helvetica* (a documentary dedicated to the font family Helvetica) was released, Nagle invited me to join him for a screening of the film in the East Village in New York City. With a detailed introduction to the film and the opportunity to ask questions, all of which built upon the typographic work we'd already done together, I was able to get more out of the film than if I had no background in typography or, more importantly, hadn't seen it with Joe at all.

Sometimes, however, people just aren't open to learning or having new experiences, even if it's something within their zone. For professionals in the creative industries, this frustration happens all the time. For example, for Bragg the interior designer, some of her clients will only be influenced as far as they want to go (and not as far as she wants them to go). Sometimes people will have hard and set preferences, at which point the only thing left to do is defer. Curators can present a point of view, but in the end they can't change clients' zone of proximal development.

It's also possible that the stubborn person has a small zone as well. Someone with a small zone might say such things as "white bread is the best kind of bread," not because the person had sampled hundreds and arrived at that conclusion; rather, it's all they've ever had, and everything else seems foreign. Someone with a large zone might also think that white bread is the best (zone size doesn't determine preferences). But because they've been sampling breads from around the world for years, they're actually ready to appreciate injera, the fermented Ethiopian flatbread.

The shape of one's zone impacts which new experiences and knowledge are within reach as well. For example, two people visit Disney World, and the first returns home excited about roller coaster design, mechanical engineering, and Newtonian physics; the shape of this person's zone was much more geared toward the machinery of the amusement park. The second person returns home excited about fantasy literature, fairy tales, and Aesop's Fables; the shape of this person's zone was directed more toward the literary aspect of the park. As Vygotsky observes, "The two children . . . displayed the same mental age from the viewpoint of developmental cycles already completed, but the developmental dynamics of the two were entirely different. The state of a child's mental development can be determined only by clarifying its two level: the actual developmental level and the zone of proximal development."[7] In other words, the zone of proximal development teaches us that there's more than just learning what one knows or expects in the present (as with the horizon of expectations). It's just as critical to observe what one is capable of learning or experiencing next.

As a result, consider that your audience is likely simultaneously composed of people appreciating your work or product right now and people who, with a little help, can come to appreciate it (and possibly buy it as a result). Do you have a strategy to reach this group? For example, a clothing store that hangs its clothes on the rack asks customers to imagine how the outfit will look. For people already capable of visualizing outfits, this works fine. For others, a mannequin modeling the clothes may be necessary to demonstrate the new pieces. For other's still, they may need to consult their friends, magazine photos, or a sales associate to decide if they like the item. Stores that can provide helpful influences will be positioned to positively engage people's zone of proximal development.

Conclusion

In an era when software, artificial intelligence, and robotics continue to automate jobs, curation (and subjectivity as a whole) remains an exclusively human endeavor. It's also one of the largest humanizing forces in today's hyperrational efficiency-focused global economy, bringing wonder, delight, and aesthetic diversity into the way we buy, sell, and make everything. And it's obvious that we need it. Everywhere online and in global commerce today, there are massive problems resulting from both the constant pressure of information overload and the loss of trust.

The problems stem from an insufficient grasp of human subjectivity and curation specifically. From search engines to social networks to recommendation engines, there's an acute lack of curation in their design, strategy, and overall business. As a result, despite the many innovative ways these technologies harness human subjectivity, they remain largely deficient in what consumers, the marketplace, and even democracy need today.

With mainstream consumers curating more of their lives online and offline (and forward-looking businesses curating as well), tolerance for untargeted, impersonal discovery experiences is evaporating. Simultaneously, awareness and sensitivities around cultural diversity have never been higher. A curation strategy addresses both of these challenges, requiring at its core diverse, subjective representation across product design, development, marketing, and advertising. The writing is on the wall for the status quo.

Like previous forms of subjectivity, curation can be harnessed. Whether it's publishing a video on YouTube, curating shoes on Pinterest, or designing a new necklace to sell on Etsy, the concepts, principles, and practices discussed in this book can drive disciplined, curation-centric strategy for connecting content with relevant audiences. A problem (and opportunity) this large won't remain unsolved forever. The story of Internet giants such as Google and Facebook is one of leveraging subjectivity to make products more useful than software alone. That opportunity exists again in curation, with tremendous possibilities for anyone who can successfully leverage it in their business, whether it be an entrepreneur founding the next Facebook, a marketer launching world-class advertising campaigns, or a creator developing products that delight audiences with heretofore unseen consistency and levels of wonder. Curation today is still the Wild West, with a chance for everyone to explore its potential. As the $2.2 trillion creative industry reorganizes around the curator class, there will be many who rise with them. Will you?

Notes

Introduction to Part I

1. O'Reilly, "Web 2.0 Expo NY: Clay Shirky (shirky.com) It's Not Information Overload. It's Filter Failure," YouTube, September 19, 2008, http://youtu.be /LabqeJEOQyI?t=23m17s.

Chapter 1

1. Larry M. Elkin, "Search Engines Help You Find the Right Needle," Palisades Hudson Financial Group LLC, January 1, 1997, http://www.palisadeshudson .com/1997/01/search-engines-help-you-find-the-right-needle/.

2. Scott Rosenberg, "Let's Get This Straight: Yes, There Is a Better Search Engine," Salon, December 21, 1998, https://www.salon.com/1998/12/21/straight_44/.

3. Adam Taylor, "47 Percent of the World's Population Now Use the Internet, Study Says," *Washington Post,* November 22, 2016, https://www.washingtonpost .com/news/worldviews/wp/2016/11/22/47-percent-of-the-worlds-population -now-use-the-internet-users-study-says/.

4. "Usage of Content Languages for Websites," W3Techs: Web Technology Surveys, https://w3techs.com/technologies/overview/content_language/all.

5. "Cisco Visual Networking Index: Forecast and Methodology, 2016–2021," Cisco, https://www.cisco.com/c/en/us/solutions/collateral/service-provider/visual -networking-index-vni/complete-white-paper-c11–481360.html.

6. "Writing about Music Is Like Dancing about Architecture," Quote Investigator, http://quoteinvestigator.com/2010/11/08/writing-about-music/.

7. Barry Schwartz, "Google's Search Knows about Over 130 Trillion Pages," Search Engine Land, November 14, 2016, http://searchengineland.com/googles -search-indexes-hits-130-trillion-pages-documents-263378.

8. Barry Schwartz, "The Tyranny of Choice," *Chronicle Review* 50, no. 20 (2004): B6, http://www.hawaii.edu/offices/app/aa/ccao/tyranny_of_choice.pdf.

9. "Form 10Q," U.S. Securities and Exchange Commission, https://www.sec .gov/Archives/edgar/data/1652044/000165204418000016/googl0-qq12018.htm.

Chapter 2

1. "Number of Monthly Active Facebook Users Worldwide as of 3rd Quarter 2018 (in Millions)," Statista, https://www.statista.com/statistics/264810/number -of-monthly-active-facebook-users-worldwide/.

2. "U.S. and World Population Clock," United States Census Bureau, https:// www.census.gov/popclock/.

3. Josh Quittner, "Facebook: Movement or Business?," *Time,* July 24, 2008, http://content.time.com/time/business/article/0,8599,1826081,00.html.

4. Pete Cashmore, "How Facebook Won the Web," CNN, April 22, 2010, http:// www.cnn.com/2010/TECH/04/22/facebook.won.the.web.cashmore/index.html.

5. Lars Backstrom, "Anatomy of Facebook," Facebook, November 21, 2011, https://www.facebook.com/notes/facebook-data-team/anatomy-of-facebook /10150388519243859.

6. R. I. M. Dunbar, "Do Online Social Media Cut through the Constraints That Limit the Size of Offline Social Networks?," Royal Society Open Science, January 20, 2016, http://rsos.royalsocietypublishing.org/content/3/1/150292.

7. Josh Constine, "How Facebook News Feed Works," Techcrunch, September 6, 2016, https://techcrunch.com/2016/09/06/ultimate-guide-to-the-news-feed/.

8. Lada Adamic, "Books That Have Stayed with Us," Facebook, September 8, 2014, https://www.facebook.com/notes/facebook-data-science/books-that-have -stayed-with-us/10152511240328859/.

9. "Form S-1: Registration Statement," Securities and Exchange Commission, https://www.sec.gov/Archives/edgar/data/1326801/000119312512034517 /d287954ds1.htm.

10. Drew Olanoff, "Spotify CEO Daniel Ek Announces Facebook Integration and Statistics at F8," The Next Web, September 22, 2011, https://thenextweb.com /apps/2011/09/22/spotify-ceo-daniel-ek-announces-facebook-integration-and -statistics-at-f8/.

11. John Paul Titlow, "Here's What Spotify's New Facebook Integration Looks Like," ReadWrite, September 23, 2011, https://readwrite.com/2011/09/23/what _spotifys_new_facebook_integration_looks_like/.

12. Mike Masnick, "How Not to Make Music Social: The Way Spotify and Face- book Did It," Techdirt, September 26, 2011, https://www.techdirt.com/articles /20110926/15102916100/how-not-to-make-music-social-way-spotify-facebook -did-it.shtml.

13. Robert Andrews, "Spotify Solves Discovery by Discovering Music Ain't So Social after All," *Gigaom,* December 6, 2012, https://gigaom.com/2012/12/06 /spotify-solves-discovery-by-discovering-music-aint-so-social-after-all/.

14. Elisa Shearer and Jeffrey Gottfried, "News Use across Social Media Plat- forms 2017," Pew Research Center, September 7, 2017, http://www.journalism .org/2017/09/07/news-use-across-social-media-platforms-2017/.

15. Claire Cain Miller, "Why Twitter's C.E.O. Demoted Himself," *New York Times,* October 30, 2010, https://www.nytimes.com/2010/10/31/technology/31ev .html.

16. Saul Hansell, "What Annoys Me about Twitter," *New York Times Blog,* April 22, 2009, https://bits.blogs.nytimes.com/2009/04/22/what-annoys-me-about-twitter/.

17. "Getting Started with Twitter," Internet Archive, https://web.archive.org /web/20160705114556/https://support.twitter.com/articles/215585.

18. Yoree Koh, "Twitter's Stock Sinks Despite Growth in Revenue, Users," *Wall Street Journal,* April 29, 2014, https://www.wsj.com/articles/twitters-revenue -surges-while-user-growth-picks-up-1398802228.

19. "Getting Started with Twitter."

20. "Create a Twitter Business Profile," Twitter for Business, https://business .twitter.com/establish-your-brand-personality.

21. Jill Duffy, "How to Get More Twitter Followers—the Right Way," *PC Magazine,* August 2, 2011, https://www.pcmag.com/article2/0,2817,2389302,00.asp.

22. Vindu Goel and Mike Isaac, "Twitter's Revolving Door Spins Again," *New York Times,* July 1, 2014, https://www.nytimes.com/2014/07/02/technology/recent -leadership-changes-suggest-that-twitter-is-failing-to-find-its-footing.html.

23. Koh, "Twitter's Stock Sinks Despite Growth in Revenue, Users."

24. Jason Gilbert, "Twitter, by the Numbers," Yahoo News, September 13, 2013, https://www.yahoo.com/news/twitter-statistics-by-the-numbers-153151584 .html.

25. James Vincent, "Former Facebook Exec Says Social Media Is Ripping Apart Society," The Verge, December 11, 2017, https://www.theverge.com/2017/12/11 /16761016/former-facebook-exec-ripping-apart-society.

26. Michael Barthel et al., "The Evolving Role of News on Twitter and Facebook," Pew Research Center, July 14, 2015, http://www.journalism.org/2015/07 /14/the-evolving-role-of-news-on-twitter-and-facebook/.

27. David Bawden and Lyn Robinson, "The Dark Side of Information: Overload, Anxiety, and Other Paradoxes and Pathologies," *Journal of Information Science* 35, no. 2 (2008): 180–191.

28. "*Bambi*—Lifetime Gross: $102,247,150," Boxoffice Mojo, https://www .boxofficemojo.com/movies/?page=releases&id=bambi.htm.

29. Stephanie Wharton, "Infographic: Top 10 Visual Commerce Trends for 2018," Curalate, November 27, 2017, https://www.curalate.com/blog/top-10-visual -commerce-trends-for-2016/.

30. David Streitfeld, "'The Internet Is Broken': @ev Is Trying to Salvage It," *New York Times,* May 20, 2017, https://www.nytimes.com/2017/05/20/technology /evan-williams-medium-twitter-internet.html.

31. Ibid.

32. Ibid.

33. Renee Diresta, "Up Next: A Better Recommendation System," *Wired,* April 11, 2018, https://www.wired.com/story/creating-ethical-recommendation-engines/.

34. Ibid.

35. Ibid.

36. Zeynep Tufekci, "YouTube, the Great Radicalizer," *New York Times,* March 10, 2018, https://www.nytimes.com/2018/03/10/opinion/sunday/youtube-politics -radical.html.

37. Ibid.

38. Ibid.

39. Jonathan L. Herlocker et al., *ACM Transactions on Information Systems* 22, no. 1 (January 2004): 5–53, http://citeseerx.ist.psu.edu/viewdoc/download?doi =10.1.1.97.5270&rep=rep1&type=pdf.

40. "Netflix Prize," Netflix, https://www.netflixprize.com/.

41. Clive Thompson, "If You Liked This, You're Sure to Love That," *New York Times Magazine,* November 21, 2008, https://www.nytimes.com/2008/11/23 /magazine/23Netflix-t.html.

42. Xavier Amatriain, "Mining Large Streams of User Data for Personalized Recommendations," *SIGKDD Explorations* 14, no. 2 (2013), http://www.kdd.org /exploration_files/V14–02-05-Amatriain.pdf.

43. Ibid.

44. Paul Sawers, "Remember Netflix's $1m Algorithm Contest? Well, Here's Why It Didn't Use the Winning Entry," The Next Web, April 13, 2012, https:// thenextweb.com/media/2012/04/13/remember-netflixs-1m-algorithm-contest -well-heres-why-it-didnt-use-the-winning-entry/.

45. Ryan Holiday, "What the Failed $1M Netflix Prize Says about Business Advice," *Forbes,* April 16, 2012, https://www.forbes.com/sites/ryanholiday/2012 /04/16/what-the-failed-1m-netflix-prize-tells-us-about-business-advice/#6110b 37d73c9.

46. Daniel M. Fleder and Kartik Hosanagar, "Blockbuster Culture's Next Rise or Fall: The Impact of Recommender Systems on Sales Diversity," *Management Science* 55, no. 5 (May 2009): 697–712, http://papers.ssrn.com/sol3/Papers. cfm?abstract_id=955984.

47. Daniel Fleder, Kartik Hosanagar, and Andreas Buja, "Recommender Systems and Their Effects on Consumers: The Fragmentation Debate," Net Institute, Working Paper 08-44, March 2010, http://econpapers.repec.org/paper/netwpaper /0844.htm.

48. Todd C. Frankel, "Why Almost No One Is Making a Living on You-Tube," *Washington Post,* March 2, 2018, https://www.washingtonpost.com/news /the-switch/wp/2018/03/02/why-almost-no-one-is-making-a-living-on-youtube/.

Chapter 3

1. Ferdinand De Saussure, *Course in General Linguistics* (New York: McGraw-Hill, 1916), 117.

2. Paul Kay and Luisa Maffi, "Color Appearance and the Emergence and Evolution of Basic Color Lexicons," *American Anthropologist* 101, no. 4 (December 1999): 744.

3. Guy Deutscher, *Through the Language Glass* (New York: Metropolitan Books, 2010), 56.

4. Anna Alberda, "Which Came First, Orange the Colour or Orange the Fruit?," *The Guardian,* March 30, 2010, https://www.theguardian.com/theguardian/2010/mar/31/origin-of-the-orange.

5. David Hume, *The Standard of Taste from Four Essays* (London: A. Millar in the Strand, 1757), 9.

6. "How Many Boards Should I Have?," BoardBooster Labs, August 2, 2015, https://boardbooster.com/labs/ideal-number-of-boards-on-your-pinterest-account/.

7. Matthew Lynley, "Pinterest Now Lets You Create Sections within Your Boards to Further Tidy Up Ideas," Techcrunch, November 9, 2017, https://techcrunch.com/2017/11/09/pinterest-now-lets-you-create-sections-within-your-boards-to-further-tidy-up-ideas/.

8. David Cohen, "Pinterest Now Has a New Way for Users to Organize Their Pins," *Adweek,* November 13, 2017, https://www.adweek.com/digital/pinterest-board-sections/.

9. William Gibson, "Broadband Blues," *The Economist,* June 21, 2001, https://www.economist.com/business/2001/06/21/broadband-blues.

10. Matt Rosoff, "Holy SMOKE! Pinterest Is the Fastest Growing Site Ever," Business Insider, February 7, 2012, https://www.businessinsider.com/holy-smoke-pinterest-is-the-fastest-growing-site-ever-2012-2.

11. Erin Griffith, "The Great Pinterestification: How Pinterest's Design Legacy Might Trump the Company Itself," Pando, September 7, 2012, https://pando.com/2012/09/07/the-great-pinterestification-how-pinterests-design-legacy-might-trump-the-company-itself/.

Introduction to Part II

1. United Nations, *Creative Economy Report 2010,* http://unctad.org/en/Docs/ditctab20103_en.pdf.

2. Anthony Ha, "The New York Times Acquires Influencer Marketing Agency HelloSociety," Techcrunch, March 11, 2016, https://techcrunch.com/2016/03/11/new-york-times-acquires-hellosociety/.

3. "HelloSociety," Crunchbase, https://www.crunchbase.com/organization/hellosociety#section-overview; Brittany Johnston, "Career over Coffee: Kyla Brennan Founder of HelloSociety," 24Seven Talent, https://www.24seventalent.com/blog/2017/01/20/career-over-coffee-kyla-brennan-founder-of-hellosociety/.

4. Debra Eckerling, "LA Tech Spotlight: Kyla Brennan, Founder, HelloSociety," *Adweek,* November 22, 2013, https://www.adweek.com/digital/la-tech-spotlight-kyla-brennan-founder-hellosociety/.

5. Ibid.

6. Ibid.

7. "HelloSociety Clients," HelloSociety, https://hellosociety.com/clients.

8. Hans Tung, "Beyond Amazon and Alibaba: What's Next for E-Commerce?" Techcrunch, August 20, 2017, https://techcrunch.com/2017/08/20/beyond-amazon-and-alibaba-whats-next-for-e-commerce/.

9. Ibid.

10. Ibid.

Chapter 4

1. Mindy Hu, "HelloInterview—Lauren Zwanziger—Pinterest 'It' Girl and Emerging Fashion Icon," Internet Archive, February 28, 2013, https://web.archive .org/web/20150926053452/https://hellosociety.com/blog/hellointerview-lauren -zwanziger-pinterest-it-girl-and-emerging-fashion-icon/.

2. Zoe Waldron, "HelloInterview: Meet Shayla Moller—Designer, World Traveler and Pinterest Influencer," Internet Archive, June 15, 2015, https://web .archive.org/web/20170927013118/https://hellosociety.com/blog/hellointerview -meet-shayla-moller-designer-world-traveler-and-pinterest-influencer/.

3. Zoe Waldron, "HelloInterview: Meet Amy Sia—Fashion & Textile Print Designer and Pinterest Influencer!," Internet Archive, May 11, 2015, https://web .archive.org/web/20160815212554/http://hellosociety.com/blog/hellointerview -meet-amy-sia-fashion-textile-print-designer-and-pinterest-influencer/.

4. Zoe Waldron, "HelloInterview: Meet Astrid Campos—Designer, Founder of Aesthete Curator, and Pinterest Influencer!," Internet Archive, April 20, 2015, https://web.archive.org/web/20171029154011/https://hellosociety.com/blog /hellointerview-meet-astrid-campos-designer-founder-of-aesthete-curator-and -pinterest-influencer/.

5. Zoe Waldron, "HelloInterview: Meet Helena Casanovas—Kids' Design Blogger and Pinterest Influencer from Barcelona!," Internet Archive, February 16, 2015, https://web.archive.org/web/20171027193618/https://hellosociety.com /blog/hellointerview-meet-helena-casanovas-kids-design-blogger-and-pinterest -influencer-from-barcelona/.

6. "Pinterest 100 2018," Pinterest Business, https://business.pinterest.com /sub/business/business-infographic-download/Pinterest-100-2018.pdf.

7. Katrina G, "CB2 and Designer Ross Cassidy Help Pinners Dream Up New Décor," Pinterest Business, March 17, 2017, https://business.pinterest.com/en /blog/cb2-and-designer-ross-cassidy-help-pinners-dream-up-new-decor.

8. Pamela Riemenschneider, "Trend Spotter: Did Jackfruit Peak?," Produce Retailer, May 29, 2018, https://www.produceretailer.com/article/news-article /trend-spotter-did-jackfruit-peak.

9. Jeffrey Gottfried and Elisa Shearer, "News Use across Social Media Platforms 2016," Pew Research Center, May 26, 2016, http://www.journalism.org /2016/05/26/news-use-across-social-media-platforms-2016/.

10. Farhad Manjoo, "Social Media's Globe-Shaking Power," *New York Times,* November 16, 2016, https://www.nytimes.com/2016/11/17/technology/social -medias-globe-shaking-power.html.

11. The Editorial Board, "Facebook and the Digital Virus Called Fake News," *New York Times,* November 19, 2016, https://www.nytimes.com/2016/11/20 /opinion/sunday/facebook-and-the-digital-virus-called-fake-news.html.

12. David Leonhardt, "Facebook's Damage to Democracy," *New York Times,* November 16, 2016, https://www.nytimes.com/2016/11/16/opinion/facebook-vs -thomas-jefferson.html.

13. Gardiner Harris and Melissa Eddy, "Obama, with Angela Merkel in Berlin, Assails Spread of Fake News," *New York Times,* November 17, 2016, https:// www.nytimes.com/2016/11/18/world/europe/obama-angela-merkel-donald -trump.html.

14. Will Oremus, "Trending Bad," Slate, August 30, 2016, http://www.slate .com/articles/technology/future_tense/2016/08/how_facebook_s_trending _news_feature_went_from_messy_to_disastrous.html.

15. Michael Nunez, "Former Facebook Workers: We Routinely Suppressed Conservative News," Gizmodo, May 9, 2016, https://gizmodo.com/former-facebook -workers-we-routinely-suppressed-conser-1775461006.

16. Brian Hughes, "How to Fix the Fake News Problem," CNN, November 16, 2016, https://www.cnn.com/2016/11/16/opinions/how-to-fix-the-fake-news -problem-hughes/index.html.

17. Anthony Ha, "The New York Times Acquires Influencer Marketing Agency HelloSociety," Techcrunch, March 11, 2016, https://techcrunch.com/2016/03/11 /new-york-times-acquires-hellosociety/.

18. Oremus, "Trending Bad."

19. Steven Bertoni, "How Spotify Made Lorde a Pop Superstar," *Forbes,* November 26, 2013, https://www.forbes.com/sites/stevenbertoni/2013/11/26 /how-spotify-made-lorde-a-pop-superstar/.

20. David Pierce, "The Secret Hit-Making Power of the Spotify Playlist," *Wired,* May 3, 2017, https://www.wired.com/2017/05/secret-hit-making-power -spotify-playlist/.

21. Cherie Hu, "Millions of Followers? Yes, But Some Top Spotify Playlists Fall Short on Engagement," *Billboard,* July 3, 2018, https://www.billboard.com /articles/business/8463174/spotify-playlists-engagement-analysis-study.

22. Peter Kafka, "Watch What Happens When Spotify Gives Unknown Music Acts a Big Push," Recode, March 28, 2017, https://www.recode.net/2017/3 /28/15079992/spotify-playlist-awal-michael-brun-gourdan-banks.

23. Sarah Perez, "Ebay Acquires 'Content Meets Commerce' Shopping Site, Bureau of Trade, As Its Personalization Efforts Heat Up," Techcrunch, September 27, 2013, https://techcrunch.com/2013/09/27/ebay-acquires-mens-content-meets -commerce-shopping-site-bureau-of-trade/.

24. K. K. Rebecca Lai and Jasmine C. Lee, "Box Office Hit or Best Picture at the Oscars? You Can Rarely Have Both," *New York Times,* March 4, 2018, https:// www.nytimes.com/interactive/2018/03/03/movies/oscars-best-picture-box -office.html.

25. Ibid.

26. Bradley Johnson, "10 Things You Should Know about the Global Ad Market," Ad Age, December 8, 2013, http://adage.com/article/global-news/10-things -global-ad-market/245572/.

27. "Rich Media Showcase," Google Rich Media Gallery, http://www.richme-diagallery.com/learn/benchmarks.

28. Tori Stark, "Why Influencers with Smaller Audiences Are the Best for Your Brand's Holiday Campaign," Internet Archive, October 25, 2016, https://web .archive.org/web/20170621004821/https://hellosociety.com/blog/why-influencers -with-smaller-audiences-are-the-best-for-your-brands-holiday-campaign/.

29. "The Remarkable Rise of Influencer Marketing [Infographic]," Influencer Marketing Hub, 2017, https://influencermarketinghub.com/the-rise-of-influencer -marketing/.

30. Farhad Manjoo, "Fall of the Banner Ad: The Monster That Swallowed the Web," *New York Times,* November 5, 2014, https://www.nytimes.com/2014/11/06 /technology/personaltech/banner-ads-the-monsters-that-swallowed-the-web .html.

31. *The Rise of Adblocking,* PageFair, August 2013, https://downloads.pagefair. com/wp-content/uploads/2016/05/The-Rise-of-Adblocking.pdf.

32. Erin Griffith, "Pandora Learns the Cost of Ads, and of Subscriptions," *Wired,* April 30, 2018, https://www.wired.com/story/pandora-learns-the-cost-of-ads-and -of-subscriptions/.

33. Lucas Shaw, "YouTube Will 'Frustrate' Some Users with Ads So They Pay for Music," Bloomberg, March 21, 2018, https://www.bloomberg.com/news /articles/2018-03-21/youtube-to-frustrate-some-users-with-ads-so-they-pay-for -music.

34. Griffith, "Pandora Learns the Cost of Ads, and of Subscriptions."

Chapter 5

1. Michelle Castillo, "This 32-Year-Old Leveraged 3.7 Million Pinterest Followers to Remodel and Furnish Her Tiny House," CNBC, November 19, 2017, https://www.cnbc.com/2017/11/19/joanna-hawley-jojotastic-pinterest-tiny -home-remodel.html.

2. Jason Del Rey, "Houzz Will Be Valued at around $4 Billion in a New Fund-ing Round Led by Iconiq Capital," Recode, June 9, 2017, https://www.recode .net/2017/6/9/15766884/houzz-4-billion-valuation-iconiq-capital-400-million -series-e-funding.

3. Sabina Leonelli, "Open Data: Curation Is Under-Resourced," *Nature* 538, no. 41 (October 6, 2016), https://www.nature.com/articles/538041d.

4. Ibid.

5. Paul Ford, "Netflix and Google Books Are Blurring the Line between Past and Present," *Wired,* February 2014, https://www.wired.com/2014/02/history/.

6. Farhad Manjoo, "Spotify Wants Listeners to Break Down Music Barriers," *New York Times,* June 3, 2015, https://www.nytimes.com/2015/06/04/technology /personaltech/spotify-sees-a-future-where-music-genres-dont-really-matter.html.

7. Lee Rainie et al., "The Rise of E-Reading," Pew Internet, April 4, 2012, http://libraries.pewinternet.org/2012/04/04/part-2-the-general-reading-habits -of-americans/.

8. "Fascinating Facts," Library of Congress, https://www.loc.gov/about/fascinating-facts/.

9. Chris Pemberton, "Gartner CMO Spend Survey 2016–2017 Shows Marketing Budgets Continue to Climb," Gartner, December 12, 2016, https://www.gartner.com/smarterwithgartner/gartner-cmo-spend-survey-2016-2017-shows-marketing-budgets-continue-to-climb/.

10. Chris Molanphy, "The Music Club, 2014," Slate, http://www.slate.com/articles/arts/the_music_club/features/2014/slate_music_club_2014/billboard_no_1_hits_2014_from_taylor_swift_to_pharrell_to_iggy_azalea_this.html.

11. Jonathan Corum, "Is That Dress White and Gold or Blue and Black?," *New York Times,* February 27, 2015, https://www.nytimes.com/interactive/2015/02/28/science/white-or-blue-dress.html.

Chapter 6

1. Alex Wilheim, "Unpacking Pinterest's $150M Series Whatever," Techcrunch, June 9, 2017, https://techcrunch.com/2017/06/09/unpacking-pinterests-150m-series-whatever/; Yoree Koh, "Pinterest Works to Pin Down Path to Wider International Audience," *Wall Street Journal,* March 23, 2016, https://www.wsj.com/articles/pinterest-works-to-pin-down-path-to-wider-international-audience-1458725401.

2. Matthew Panzarino, "Costolo Says Twitter's Future Is More Curation, Relevance and Media," Techcrunch, https://techcrunch.com/2015/05/28/costolo-says-twitters-future-is-more-curation-relevance-and-media/.

3. Sarah Perez, "Twitter Finally Lets Everyone Create Their Own 'Moments,'" Techcrunch, September 28, 2016, https://techcrunch.com/2016/09/28/twitter-finally-lets-everyone-create-their-own-moments/.

4. Ben Woods, "Google Now Lets You Save Image Search Results to Your Account," The Next Web, December 11, 2015, https://thenextweb.com/google/2015/12/11/google-now-lets-you-save-image-search-results-to-your-account/.

5. Sarah Perez, "Ebay Acquires 'Content Meets Commerce' Shopping Site, Bureau of Trade, as Its Personalization Efforts Heat Up," Techcrunch, September 27, 2013, https://techcrunch.com/2013/09/27/ebay-acquires-mens-content-meets-commerce-shopping-site-bureau-of-trade/.

6. Erin Griffith, "eBay: Forget Auctions, We Are All about Curated Boutiques. (Just Like Everyone Else)," PandoDaily, October 22, 2013, https://pando.com/2013/10/22/ebay-forget-auctions-we-are-all-about-curated-boutiques-just-like-everyone-else/.

7. "Fab," Crunchbase, https://www.crunchbase.com/organization/fab-com; Diana Budds, "Bradford Shellhammer's Next Project: Curating eBay," Fast Company, March 25, 2016, https://www.fastcompany.com/3058286/bradford-shellhammers-next-project-curating-ebay.

8. Budds, "Bradford Shellhammer's Next Project."

9. Anthony Ha, "The New York Times Acquires Influencer Marketing Agency HelloSociety," Techcrunch, March 11, 2016, https://techcrunch.com/2016/03/11/new-york-times-acquires-hellosociety/.

10. Jeremy Barr, "Mark Thompson at SXSW: Why the New York Times Bought HelloSociety," Ad Age, March 12, 2016, http://adage.com/article/special-report -sxsw/mark-thompson-york-times-bought-hellosociety/303088/.

11. Sheila Dang, "New York Times Launches Digital Subscriptions for Cooking Site," Reuters, June 28, 2017, https://www.reuters.com/article/us-new-york-times -cooking/new-york-times-launches-digital-subscriptions-for-cooking-site -idUSKBN19J2TE.

12. Katie Zhu, "Collections: Curating a More Browsable Medium," Medium, March 15, 2016, https://blog.medium.com/collections-curating-a-more-browsable -medium-562f7ff9a617.

13. "Medium," Crunchbase, https://www.crunchbase.com/organization /medium.

14. Zhu, "Collections."

15. Reggie Ugwu, "Inside the Playlist Factory," BuzzFeed, July 12, 2016, https://www.buzzfeed.com/reggieugwu/the-unsung-heroes-of-the-music -streaming-boom.

16. Jordan Crook, "Google Buys Songza," Techcrunch, July 1, 2014, https:// techcrunch.com/2014/07/01/google-buys-songza/.

17. Alex Heath, "Apple Thinks Human Editors Will Be the Key to Its Music Service's Success," Business Insider, August 7, 2015, https://www.businessinsider .com/jimmy-iovine-on-apple-music-curation-2015-8.

18. Jillian D'Onfro, "Tim Cook Says He Couldn't Sleep the Night after Listening to Beats Radio for the First Time," Business Insider, September 12, 2014, https://www.businessinsider.com/tim-cook-on-why-apple-bought-beats -2014-9.

19. Sarah Perez, "Apple Revamps the App Store's Games Section with Increased Focus on Editorial Content," Techcrunch, June 1, 2015, https://techcrunch .com/2015/06/01/apple-revamps-the-app-stores-games-section-with-increased -focus-on-editorial-content/.

20. Sam Costello, "How Many Apps Are in the App Store?" Lifewire, April 7, 2018, https://www.lifewire.com/how-many-apps-in-app-store-2000252.

21. Sarah Perez, "Majority of U.S. Consumers Still Download Zero Apps per Month, Says Comscore," Techcrunch, August 25, 2017, https://techcrunch .com/2017/08/25/majority-of-u-s-consumers-still-download-zero-apps-per -month-says-comscore/; Sarah Perez, "Apple's Huge App Store Makeover Arrives Today in iOS 11," Techcrunch, September 19, 2017, https://techcrunch. com/2017/09/19/apples-huge-app-store-makeover-arrives-today-in-ios-11/.

22. Perez, "Apple's Huge App Store Makeover Arrives Today in iOS 11."

23. "VSCO," Crunchbase, https://www.crunchbase.com/organization/visual -supply-co-vsco#/entity.

24. Dan Seifert, "VSCO Now Has 30 Million Active Users," The Verge, January 14, 2016, https://www.theverge.com/2016/1/14/10767142/vsco-30-million-users.

25. Lydia Dishman, "VSCO Cam, the Anti-Instagram, Is the Future of Mobile Photography," Fast Company, August 13, 2013, https://www.fastcompany.com /3015537/vsco-cam-the-anti-instagram-is-the-future-of-mobile-photography.

26. "VSCO," Craft, https://craft.co/vsco.

27. Ilyse Liffreing, "How PowerBar Is Using Photography App VSCO to Find Talent," Digiday, March 2, 2018, https://digiday.com/marketing/powerbar -using-photography-app-vsco-find-talent/.

28. Ibid.

29. Bridget Schneider, "Photography App VSCO Could Lead to Your Big Break," Resource, March 4, 2018, http://resourcemagonline.com/2018/03/photography -app-vsco-could-lead-to-your-big-break/86735/.

30. Debra Eckerling, "LA Tech Spotlight: Kyla Brennan, Founder, Hello-Society," *Adweek,* November 22, 2013, https://www.adweek.com/digital/la-tech -spotlight-kyla-brennan-founder-hellosociety/.

31. Ibid.

32. Michelle Castillo, "This 32-Year-Old Leveraged 3.7 Million Pinterest Followers to Remodel and Furnish Her Tiny House," CNBC, November 19, 2017, https://www.cnbc.com/2017/11/19/joanna-hawley-jojotastic-pinterest-tiny -home-remodel.html.

Chapter 7

1. Zoe Waldron, "HelloInterview: Meet Jillian Tohber Leslie—Founder of Catch My Party and a Pinterest Influencer," Internet Archive, June 22, 2015, https://web.archive.org/web/20170927062729/https://hellosociety.com/blog /hellointerview-meet-jillian-leslie-founder-of-catch-my-party-and-a-pinterest -influencer/.

2. "National Design Awards," Cooper Hewitt, https://www.cooperhewitt.org /national-design-awards/.

3. Steward Rogers, "Study Shows 99% of Organic Social Posts Create Almost No Engagement," VentureBeat, August 19, 2014, https://venturebeat.com/2014/08/19 /study-shows-99-of-organic-social-posts-create-almost-no-engagement/.

4. Ricardo Bilton, "Publishers Have an Updated Evergreen Strategy: Make the Old New Again," Digiday, July 16, 2014, https://digiday.com/media/publishers -evergreen-content-strategy-make-the-old-new-again/.

5. Christian Zappone, "Iowa 'Futures' Show Republican Weakness," CNN Money, October 11, 2006, https://money.cnn.com/2006/10/11/news/economy /markets_congress/.

6. Ajit Kambil, "You Can Bet on Idea Markets," Harvard Business School Working Knowledge, December 1, 2003, https://hbswk.hbs.edu/archive/you-can -bet-on-idea-markets.

7. Walt Hickey, "Betting Markets (Mostly) Nailed the Oscar Nominations," FiveThirtyEight, January 15, 2015, https://fivethirtyeight.com/features /betting-markets-mostly-nailed-the-oscar-nominations/.

8. Kambil, "You Can Bet on Idea Markets."

9. Mark Harris, "Shorting Tinseltown," *New York Magazine,* July 25, 2010, http://nymag.com/movies/theindustry/67275/.

10. Daniel Grant, "How to Say 'No Thanks' to Donors," *Wall Street Journal,* May 19, 2010, https://www.wsj.com/articles/SB1000142405270230422250457 5173803616852666.

11. Tori Stark, "HelloInterview: Catching Up with Jillian Tohber Leslie, Founder of Catch My Party," Internet Archive, September 1, 2016, https://web .archive.org/web/20170620152308/https://hellosociety.com/blog/hellointerview -catching-up-with-jillian-tohber-leslie-founder-of-catch-my-party/.

12. Ibid.

13. Emily Zulz, "Are You a Contrarian or Part of the Herd?," ThinkAdvisor, May 5, 2015, https://www.thinkadvisor.com/2015/05/05/are-you-a-contrarian -or-part-of-the-herd.

Chapter 8

1. Mary M. Long and Leon G. Schiffman, "Swatch Fever: An Allegory for Understanding the Paradox of Collecting," *Psychology & Marketing* 14, no. 5 (August 1997): 495–509.

2. Ibid., 502.

3. Ibid., 504.

4. Gery W. Ryan and H. Russell Bernard, "Techniques to Identify Themes," *Field Methods* 15, no. 1 (2003): 85–109.

5. Zoe Waldron, "Guest Post: Katherine Accettura's Top 5 Pinterest Tips," Internet Archive, May 27, 2015, https://web.archive.org/web/20170926145748 /https://hellosociety.com/blog/guest-post-katherine-accetturas-top-5-pinterest -influencer-training-tips/.

6. Zoe Waldron, "HelloInterview: Meet Holly Menard—Mom and Pinterest Influencer from the South!," Internet Archive, May 4, 2015, https://web.archive .org/web/20170927015131/https://hellosociety.com/blog/hellointerview-meet -holly-menard-mom-and-pinterest-influencer-from-the-south/.

7. Zoe Waldron, "HelloInterview: Meet Rowena Murillo—Writer, Teacher and Pinterest Influencer!," Internet Archive, May 25, 2015, https://web.archive .org/web/20160815214337/http://hellosociety.com/blog/hellointerview-meet -rowena-murillo-writer-teacher-and-pinterest-influencer/.

8. Long and Schiffman, "Swatch Fever," 502.

9. Waldron, "HelloInterview: Meet Rowena Murillo."

10. Thor Kell and George Tzanetakis, "Empirical Analysis of Track Selection and Ordering in Electronic Dance Music Using Audio Feature Extraction," International Society for Music Information Retrieval, 2012, http://www.ppgia.pucpr .br/ismir2013/wp-content/uploads/2013/09/210_Paper.pdf.

11. The Associated Press, "Connecticut Hoarder Dies after First Floor Collapses under Weight of Clutter," *New York Daily News,* June 15, 2014, http://www.nydaily news.com/news/national/hoarder-dies-floor-falls-basement-article-1.1830924.

Chapter 9

1. Brenda Danet and Tamar Katriel, "No Two Alike: Play and Aesthetics in Collecting," *Play and Culture* 2, no. 3 (1989): 255–271.

2. Catherine Carey, "Modeling Collecting Behavior: The Role of Set Completion," *Journal of Economic Psychology* 29 (2008): 336–347.

3. Danet and Katriel, "No Two Alike."

4. Carey, "Modeling Collective Behavior."

5. Ryan Tate, "This Is the Perfect Pinterest Picture according to Science," *Wired*, June 4, 2013, https://www.wired.com/2013/06/this-is-the-perfect-pinterest-picture/.

6. Russell Belk et al., "Collecting in a Consumer Culture," in *SV—Highways and Buyways: Naturalistic Research from the Consumer Behavior Odyssey*, ed. Russell Belk, 178–215 (Provo, UT: Association for Consumer Research, 1991), http://acrwebsite.org/volumes/12102/volumes/sv06/SV-06.

7. Tate, "This Is the Perfect Pinterest Picture according to Science."

Chapter 10

1. Josh Sanburn, "Why the Death of Malls Is about More Than Shopping," *Time*, July 20, 2017, http://time.com/4865957/death-and-life-shopping-mall/.

2. Shelly Banjo and Drew FitzGerald, "Stores Confront New World of Reduced Shopper Traffic," *Wall Street Journal*, January 16, 2014, https://www.wsj.com/articles/stores-confront-new-world-of-reduced-shopper-traffic-1389919360.

3. Gene Weingarten, "Pearls before Breakfast: Can One of the Nation's Great Musicians Cut through the Fog of a D.C. Rush Hour? Let's Find Out," *Washington Post*, April 8, 2007, https://www.washingtonpost.com/lifestyle/magazine/pearls-before-breakfast-can-one-of-the-nations-great-musicians-cut-through-the-fog-of-a-dc-rush-hour-lets-find-out/2014/09/23/8a6d46da-4331-11e4-b47c-f5889e061e5f_story.html.

4. Ibid.

5. "Copyright in Derivative Works and Compilations," U.S. Copyright Office, 2013, https://www.copyright.gov/circs/circ14.pdf.

6. "Ministry of Sound Sues Spotify," BBC, September 4, 2013, https://www.bbc.com/news/entertainment-arts-23956750.

Chapter 11

1. Russell Belk, "Extended Self in a Digital World," *Journal of Consumer Research* 40, no. 3 (October 2013): 477–500.

2. Donald O. Case, "Serial Collecting as Leisure, and Coin Collecting in Particular," *Library Trends* 57, no. 4 (Spring 2009): 729–752.

3. Russell Belk et al., "Collecting in a Consumer Culture," in *SV—Highways and Buyways: Naturalistic Research from the Consumer Behavior Odyssey*, ed. Russell

Belk, 178–215 (Provo, UT: Association for Consumer Research, 1991), http://acrwebsite.org/volumes/12102/volumes/sv06/SV-06.

4. Case, "Serial Collecting."

5. Belk et al., "Collecting in a Consumer Culture."

6. Zoe Waldron, "HelloInterview: Meet Jennifer Moen—Stay-at-Home Mom and Pinterest Influencer!," Internet Archive, June 8, 2015, https://web.archive.org/web/20170927003106/https://hellosociety.com/blog/hellointerview-meet-jennifer-moen-stay-at-home-mom-and-pinterest-influencer/.

Chapter 12

1. Charlotte Bruce Harvey, "Scents + Sensibility," Brown Alumni Magazine, March/April 2008, http://www.brownalumnimagazine.com/content/view/1936/40/.

2. Ibid.

3. Priya Krishnakumar, Joe Fox, and Chris Keller, "Here's Where More Than 7,500 Buildings Were Destroyed and Damaged in California's Wine Country Fires," *Los Angeles Times,* October 25, 2017, http://www.latimes.com/projects/la-me-northern-california-fires-structures/.

4. Paul Rozin et al., "Glad to Be Sad, and Other Examples of Benign Masochism," *Judgement and Decision Making* 8, no. 4 (2013): 439–447, https://digitalcommons.wcupa.edu/musichtc_facpub/26/.

5. Erika Engelhaupt, "People Sometimes Like Stinky Things—Here's Why," *National Geographic,* August 3, 2015, https://www.nationalgeographic.com/science/phenomena/2015/08/03/why-do-people-sometimes-like-stinky-things/.

6. Rozin et al., "Glad to Be Sad."

7. George MacDonald, *What's Mine's Mine,* Vol. 2 (Boston: D. Lothrop, 1886), 163.

Chapter 13

1. "Wilhelm Maximilian Wundt," Stanford Encyclopedia of Philosophy, https://plato.stanford.edu/entries/wilhelm-wundt/.

2. K. B. Madsen, *A History of Psychology in Metascientific Perspective* (Amsterdam: Elsevier Science Publishers, 1988), 143.

3. W. Sluckin, A. M. Colman, and D. J. Hargreaves, "Liking Words as a Function of the Experienced Frequency of Their Occurrence," *British Journal of Psychology* 71 (1980): 163–169, https://www2.le.ac.uk/departments/npb/people/amc/articles-pdfs/likiword.pdf.

4. Hans Robert Jauss and Elizabeth Benzinger, "Literary History as a Challenge to Literary Theory," *A Symposium on Literary History,* special issue of *New Literary History* 2, no. 1 (Autumn 1970), 14, http://www.rlwclarke.net/Theory/SourcesPrimary/JaussLiteraryHistoryasaChallengetoLiteraryTheory.pdf.

5. Steven J. Haggbloom et al., "The 100 Most Eminent Psychologists of the 20th Century," *Review of General Psychology* 6, no. 2 (2002): 144, http://creativity .ipras.ru/texts/top100.pdf.

6. Lev S. Vygotsky, "Interaction between Learning and Development," in *Readings on the Development of Children,* ed. Mary Gauvain and Michael Cole (New York: Scientific American Books, 1978), 38.

7. Ibid., 38.

Index

An italicized f *following a page number indicates figures;* t *indicates tables.*

About the Author

Steffon Davis is a product manager working on autonomous vehicles at Uber in its Advanced Technology Group in the San Francisco Bay area. He is also founder of the curation analytics platform Curalytics. Previously, Davis worked in algorithmic foreign exchange trading for a venture-funded financial technology company and founded the social curation platform Topiat. He has also invested in start-ups as an associate with the New York Angels investment group. A graduate of Brown University, Davis advocates for an interdisciplinary approach to problem solving and consults on issues ranging from product design and fund-raising to curation strategy.